THE LORD OUR SHEPHERD

THE LORD OUR SHEPHERD

J. Douglas MacMillan

Second edition
Revised and enlarged

BRYNTIRION PRESS

EP BOOKS
First Floor Venture House, 6 Silver Court, Watchmead,
Welwyn Garden City, UK, AL7 1TS
e-mail: sales@epbooks.org
web: www.epbooks.org

EP BOOKS are distributed in the USA by:
JPL Fulfillment, 3741 Linden Avenue Southeast,
Grand Rapids, MI 49548
E-mail: sales@jplfulfillment.com
Tel: 877.683.6935

ISBN 978–1–85049–198–9

This book contains the substance of a series of addresses delivered
at the Annual Conference of the Evangelical Movement of Wales at
Aberystwyth in 1979. In this second edition, the addresses are preceded
by the author's personal testimony.

Unless otherwise stated, all Scripture quotations are from the Authorised
(King James) version.

Published by Bryntirion Press, Office Manager, Evangelical Movement
of Wales, Waterton Cross Business Park, South Road, Bridgend, CF31
3UL / Rheolwraig Swyddfa, Mudiad Efengylaidd Cymru, Waterton
Cross Business Park, South Road, Pen-y-Bont ar Ogwr, CF31 3UL.
Tel/Ffôn: 01656 655886; Website/Gwefan:www.emw.org.uk
Bryntirion Press books are published in association with EP Books.

BRYNTIRION PRESS

Contents

Foreword

TO write a commendation for a book that has been reprinted six times in the last fifteen years may seem superfluous. But its appearance in a new edition and the potential of a new readership makes the task not only appropriate but also necessary. For these and other reasons—a cherished friendship with its author among them—I am grateful to the Publishers for the invitation to write this Foreword and undertake the duty gladly.

The main part of this little book contains four sermons on Psalm 23. They were first preached at the annual conference of the Evangelical Movement of Wales in 1979 by the late Revd J. Douglas MacMillan, and published four years later under the title of *The Lord our Shepherd*. In his Foreword to that edition, the Revd Elwyn Davies, the General Secretary of the Movement, recalled how 'the congregation [had] listened spellbound' to those sermons.

Since then, many more have come to appreciate them—over 45,000 copies of that edition have been sold. In addition, it has been translated into Romanian, Spanish and Portuguese. (Audiotapes of those addresses are still available from the Publisher of this volume.)

In the last quarter of the twentieth century, the name of Douglas MacMillan became identified for many, not only within the United Kingdom but in Australia, New Zealand, South Africa and Canada, with a rare form of preaching—one marked by a powerful originality and a strong orthodoxy. These addresses on Psalm 23 are probably the clearest examples of this rare combination.

Their originality

As is well known, it was a shepherd who composed Psalm 23—hence all the imagery that it contains. The same is true with regard to these addresses. Their preacher–author spent twelve years of his life as a shepherd on the Ardnamurchan peninsula in Argyll, the most westerly part of the Scottish mainland. He knew what it was like to be out on its hills in all weathers and at all hours, caring for sheep. That day-to-day experience contributes to the uniqueness of these addresses in no small measure. But it does not wholly explain their originality.

Neither his shepherding nor his familiarity with the text of this psalm provided Douglas MacMillan with an entrance into that wonderful relationship with the Lord which is described in it. Something else was needed, and it was his being made aware that although he knew what was involved in looking after sheep, he needed a shepherd himself because he had wandered far from the fold. Born to godly parents, prayed for and brought up under the sound of the gospel, Psalm 23 was well known to him in Gaelic as well as English; but he did not know the Shepherd. How this came about is told in the early part of his testimony, whose inclusion in this volume greatly enhances the spiritual value of this book.

Also recorded there is how an earnest and caring undershepherd sought and 'penned' him—of which more later. But it was his being found by the Lord that made all the difference to him, and to his view of this Psalm. That is what makes these addresses so original. Many have preached on Psalm 23 without ever having had to look for sheep until they are found and then having to carry them all the way home. That experience gave a tangible immediacy—and it comes out so clearly in the many illustrations contained in these addresses—to his having been personally sought, found and cared for by the Good Shepherd.

Their orthodoxy

But if that is their origin, what explains their rich orthodoxy? There is more here than personal reflections on a shepherd's life in the light of a newly found Saviour. Revd MacMillan writes: 'When I came to know the Lord, I think that he drew me to [the shepherd] theme in Scripture, and I was able to interpret much of the Lord's dealings with myself from my own experience among sheep.'

These addresses are therefore the fruit of some three years of communion with Christ, the Chief Shepherd, in the light of the whole of Scripture. That laid the foundation for the eight years of serious study by way of preparation for the work of the Christian ministry, and the accurate and lively proclamation of the Word which followed it. Significantly, Douglas MacMillan said: 'I think that I had been preaching for eighteen years before I went anywhere near Psalm 23 in a pulpit'—that must mean that Psalm 23 was for him something like holy ground.

These addresses are the fruit of careful exegesis and sound theology, but they are also messages of life to Christian people. They follow the bone structure of the psalm, which is a 'he–me' relationship between the Lord and every one of his people. They also transmit its lifeblood, namely, that of being known by him and knowing him; and they identify its sinews, which are the ways in which the Shepherd cares for his own.

Here is wonderful trinitarian redemptive theology coupled with profound pastoral theology. It is no wonder that the General Assembly of the Free Church of Scotland appointed him to the Chair of Church History and Church Principles in 1982, after his pastorates at Aberdeen (1966–74) and Glasgow (1974–82). It was a just recognition of the need that its ministerial students might 'catch' something of that rare combination of truth and life, knowledge of Scripture truth and also of people, which he embodied, and which cannot really be taught.

He underwent major heart surgery in 1990 but recovered well. But on 3 August 1991 he was called home, just as he was about to return to pastoral ministry, which was probably his first love. On 9 August, the 'young preacher' to whom he refers in his testimony spoke at his funeral service in Kilchoan, Argyll. For some time previously, the Revd David Patterson had been in considerable turmoil as to what he should say to those who would gather, many of whom, he knew, were companions of Douglas in his pre-conversion days. But as he relived the close fellowship that the two of them had enjoyed over the years, a few words darted into his mind, as if from Douglas himself. They were, 'Davie, just tell them that he kept me.' That was the theme around which the message was tellingly constructed. It is, of course, where the psalm ends: 'Surely goodness and mercy shall follow me all the days of my life; and I will dwell in the house of the Lord for ever.'

What Asaph said about David at the end of Psalm 78 comes to mind as being also true of Revd Professor J. Douglas MacMillan as an under-shepherd of David's greater son:

He chose David also his servant, and took him from the sheepfolds: from following the ewes great with young he brought him to feed Jacob his people, and Israel his inheritance. So he fed them according to the integrity of his heart; and guided them by the skilfulness of his hands.

HYWEL R JONES

Professor of Practical Theology
Westminster Theological Seminary, California

Foreword
to the First Edition

ALL who attended the conference at which these addresses were delivered were immediately conscious that they were present at a unique occasion. Devoting the mornings and evenings of their summer holiday to the worship of God and to fellowship with his people, they did not need to be persuaded that it is always a privilege to sit under the ministry of God's servants. But this was different. Not only was the speaker a gifted preacher and an able expositor of the Word of God, but prior to his call to the Christian ministry he had been a shepherd for twelve years. And he had taken Psalm 23 as his theme! Expectations were aroused. And they were not to be disappointed.

Morning by morning the congregation listened spellbound as, drawing on his own experience with the sheep he had loved, the preacher illustrated the profound statements of this wonderful psalm. As he stood with arms uplifted and then, suddenly, with massive hand clasped to his chest, we felt we could almost see the lambs he would often have carried to safety. What was more important, before the end of that week we had been helped to see the Great Shepherd himself in a light that was entirely new.

The psalm had taken on a new meaning and significance. For weeks and months afterwards, those who were present would be heard repeating the anecdotes and illustrations they had heard, commenting on words they had known since childhood as though they had never heard them before.

It is a great joy therefore to see these addresses, and particularly the third and fourth addresses, appearing in print.

Christian doctrine must be translated into Christian experience, else it is arid and barren. That is the challenge, but also the comforting

possibility, that the author holds before us in these addresses. His qualifications for doing so are, we repeat, unique. His twofold role as shepherd, once of God's creatures, now of God's children, and his firsthand experience of handling both, coupled with a firm grasp of the Scriptures, a pastor's heart and a mind steeped in God's Word, eminently qualify him for the task. All who read cannot but be helped and inspired.

J. ELWYN DAVIES

I. Personal Testimony

Personal
Testimony

I was born in the County of Argyll, in the Parish of Western Ardnamurchan on the last day of September 1933. I had the great privilege of being born into a Christian home and was the youngest of six children, two girls and four boys. The most westerly point of mainland Britain, Ardnamurchan is a peninsula running into the Atlantic ocean, with the island of Skye lying to the North and the island of Mull to the South. It was in many ways an idyllic place in which to be brought up, and fostered in me a great love for the countryside and, in particular, for the sea and the mountains.

When I was a little boy, my father was a building contractor but also ran a croft, or small farm, on which the family did the work. From the earliest time I can remember, the croft animals, cows and calves, sheep and lambs, horses and, of course, collie dogs were part of our rich and varied everyday life. We did not realise it at the time, but it was a kind of life fast fading into the obscurity of history.

My father was a very hard-working, upright, honest, able man with a fine mind and a very skilful pair of hands. A deeply exercised Christian, his heart was open to all kinds of people, and he was a helper of every needy person and cause. I don't think I have ever met anyone whom I have respected in quite the same way as I respected him. He was converted in middle life, in the year 1921, when a visiting preacher held meetings in our village. He went through a long, trying period under great conviction of sin, and was hugely troubled for a time over the doctrine of election. His deliverance from all this came by way of a powerful experience of God's grace in Christ when reading a sermon on that very subject by C. H. Spurgeon.

I have counted it as a fortunate thing that, being the son of a bardic family and endowed with a fine command of good, fluent Gaelic, he has left some of his early spiritual experiences on record in the form of a few fine Gaelic spiritual songs and hymns. After his conversion he began to preach and, along with other young Christian converts of that period, to hold Cottage Meetings in the villages surrounding his home. My mother, Jessie MacLachlan, was also of Ardnamurchan people on both sides of her family, but had been born and brought up in Glasgow. She came to Ardnamurchan to care for an elderly uncle and soon afterwards was converted through hearing my father preach.

Memories of my childhood are happy ones, and many of them centre around the gospel and the love which the gospel always brings into a home. I still recall very vividly our worship times as a family, my father's prayers, and his carrying me on his shoulders as we went through the woods and over the hill tracks to the lovely white-sanded bay where the people of four little hamlets met for worship and preaching at three o'clock on Sunday afternoons. Our home often entertained the preachers or other Christians, and so I think I always knew that the Lord's people were happy and greatly enjoyed each other's fellowship.

I remember, on one occasion, sitting in that small church at Sanna Bay listening to our minister preaching on the Judgement and describing how people on that Day would call on the mountains to fall on them and cover them from the face of God. At one point in his sermon he tiptoed very gently over to the windows of this little church and, pointing upwards to where we could all see the huge, rugged, granite rocks and boulders perched on the steep slopes of the hills as they towered above us, said in a voice filled with awe, 'People will be calling on those very rocks and hills to hide them from God, if they are not ready to meet him on that great day.' I was probably only three or four years old at the time, but I can still remember feeling the power of that moment and the still, solemn hush that came over us all.

I can remember something else which had an even more vivid and lasting effect on my life, and which took place when I was eight years old. In our times of family worship we used to sing some verses of a psalm; and one Sunday evening when we were singing the opening verses of Psalm 40 I had a very powerful sense of the nearness and the love of God. As we sang, I felt something very special in these words which speak about God taking us out of the miry clay, setting our feet upon a rock, and putting a new song in our mouths. My heart was touched and melted, and I really felt that God loved me and had come to me. So I told my parents and my friends at school that I had been converted. For quite a long time after I tried to live like a Christian, at home and at school.

Outgrowing religion

When I was nearly twelve, I had to leave home to attend secondary school at Tobermory on the island of Mull. Here, two things worked against my continuing to think and act as a Christian. First of all, there were no other believers of my own age. Secondly, one of my new teachers positively undermined my faith in the Bible. By the time I was thirteen, I felt I had outgrown religion. I put behind me the impressions I had had from early childhood. Religion was all right for the likes of my parents, whom I regarded as old and old-fashioned, but it was not something which I needed.

Before I was fourteen, I had to leave school. Two years earlier, my father had moved to quite a large farm, which he ran with my two older brothers and, at certain times, help from an uncle with the sheep. My eldest brother was leaving home that autumn to study at Veterinary College in Glasgow, and at the same time I ran into difficulties finding accommodation near my school. Just as these were being overcome, in the month of January 1948, my uncle died very suddenly. And so, with pressure of work in looking after his croft, with its horse, cows and sheep, as well as the sheep on our own farm, I was, to my own entire satisfaction, allowed to abandon any further thought of returning to school almost a year before attaining the minimum leaving age and, in the event, never went back at all.

I had just got settled into this new situation and the beginning of a working teenage life when my mother, who had had surgery a year or so earlier, began to be very unwell and finally became ill with a painful terminal cancer. Strangely enough, despite her own faith and cheerfulness, her illness and especially the longdragged-out closing year of her life confirmed me in the antireligious, anti-Christian attitudes I had begun to adopt during my last year at school.

Another influence in my life at this time was the books I used to borrow from a man with Communist views (a red Clydesider), who came to live not far away. As I read these books, especially through the long wintry nights, I felt confirmed in my rejection of Christianity.

Will I meet you in heaven?

I also recall something which happened one night in the early springtime of that final year of mother's life. My brother and I had been out at a ceilidh and dance, singing and playing accordions in a village about thirty-five miles away. We got home in the wee small hours of the morning—just as a new day was beginning to break. I opened the back door of our house and immediately heard a strange but beautiful sound. It was my mother's voice. She had had some training in voice production when young and had, at one time, sung with some groups in Glasgow. But here she was now, just months before her death, and at a time when her days were often filled with great pain, awake in the middle of the night with the stress of her illness, and my father sitting with her, softly singing a glorious testimony of faith in the verses of one of her favourite psalms:

I shall not die, but live, and shall
   The works of God discover:
The Lord hath me chastisèd sore,
   But not to death giv'n over.

O set ye open unto me
   The gates of righteousness;
Then will I enter into them,
   And I the Lord will bless.   (Psalm 118:17–19)

She was singing the second verse just as my hand was on the handle of the back door. I was so overcome I could not go in. I went away up into the hills to cry. Here was I, full of youthfulness and with everything opening out before me, and there she was, so weak and in such pain, yet singing with triumph about what was opening out before her. There was something about that, and about her whole life, that touched even my hard heart. Three months later, one hot day in July, I was in my mother's room and she asked me to read a few verses for her from the Bible.

'Where would you like me to read?'

'In John chapter 14.'

I took up the Bible and began to read:

Let not your heart be troubled: ye believe in God, believe also in me. In my Father's house are many mansions: if it were not

19

so, I would have told you. I go to prepare a place for you. And if I go and prepare a place for you, I will come again, and receive you unto myself; that where I am, there ye may be also.

'That's enough.'

'But, Mam, would you not like me to read a bit more? I could read the whole chapter.' (I was actually feeling quite proud that I could do this for my mother.)

But she said, 'No, Douglas, that's enough. That's everything.' Then she turned to me and said, 'Douglas, there is something I want to say to you. I may never talk to you again. In a short time I am going to be with Jesus. But I want to ask you, Will you meet me there?'

Four days later, she died. So, seven days after that last conversation, I was standing beside my mother's grave. It was as if I could hear her voice ringing in my ears, 'Will I meet you in heaven?' I knew that if there was a heaven, I was not walking on the road that led to it. I felt I had to harden my heart against my mother's appeal, and I did.

Were you in church last Sunday?

However, there were many things which began to get to me and leave me very uneasy with my life and outlook. For example, in my work as a shepherd I was closely in touch with nature. Especially in lambing time, I had to get up when it was dark and climb the hills as day was dawning. From the height of the mountains behind our house, the beauty of nature was staggering.

I remember sitting down on the top of a mountain early one morning, and looking out to the west. I could see the nearer islands and, beyond them, the Outer Hebrides. Beyond that, there was nothing between me and America. The beauty and immensity of everything made my hair stand on end. I could not get the question out of my head—Where did all this come from? To cut a long story short, six or seven years of atheism came to an end, as I found it actually easier to accept the existence of God than to go on believing that all this beauty and order came from nothing.

But now a new struggle started. What if the God who made the world was the same God as my parents believed in? What if the Bible was true? What if there was a heaven and a hell? I remember that as I was out drinking one evening, I was suddenly overcome by the seriousness of a question from which I could not escape: What if all I had been taught about the Bible was true?

One night, when I was in a local pub, a man asked me, 'Douglas, were you in church last Sunday?' I said, 'No—not me! These fellows just put me to sleep.'

A week later I was playing my accordion at a dance. I got up to dance with a girl, and as we moved round the floor together she suddenly asked me, 'Douglas, were you in church last Sunday?' I was beginning to feel persecuted! But she went on: 'There's a wonderful young preacher. You must go and hear him.' I'll not repeat what I said to her.

The mask removed

My older brother used to drive my father to the midweek service in the church six or seven miles away. But, one Wednesday around that time, my brother was away at a cattle sale and I got the job of driving my father to the church. I intended, while he was in the church, going to the pub for a drink and then going to visit a girl. However, as we came near to the church I had an idea. I asked my father, 'Who will be preaching tonight? Is it that young preacher?'

'Yes.'

I thought, 'This is my chance to find out what they are all talking about.' I went in with my father, but as soon as I sat down in the church amongst these old people I began to wonder if I was going mad. What if my mates found out that I spent my Wednesday evening in a church?

Then the door behind the pulpit opened, and I got quite a shock. I thought that all preachers were old men, ready to crumble and fall into the grave. They were religious because there was nothing better for them to do. But this young man was just a little older than I was myself. He looked as if he had a broken nose—in fact his whole appearance reminded me of my hero Freddie Mills, the British cruiserweight boxer who was then champion of the world.

At first I was disappointed when he began to speak. His voice was low, as if he was afraid of all the old ladies in black. His text was: 'Because thou sayest, I am rich, and increased in goods, and have need of nothing; and knowest not that thou art wretched, and miserable, and poor, and blind, and naked: I counsel thee to buy of me gold tried in the fire ...' (Revelation 3:17–18). To this day I am amazed that he chose to speak on a text like that, when he must have expected to be addressing a group of old Christians. Anyway he described what he found in the text—the spectacle of a soul worshipping itself.

What took my breath away was that he gave an exact description of me and of my life. I was living for myself, for pleasure and for what I could accomplish. I drank, I enjoyed the company of the lassies, but there were also hard ambitions which had taken over my life. I lived for money. And there was another thing: I used to do the round of the Highland Games, and often featured in the prize lists for the 'Heavy Events'. I was especially keen on hammer-throwing. I had been doing it since I was fifteen and thought that in about four years I could reach the top.

But as I listened to the preacher in that quiet country church, all these things lost their dazzle. The very things which had become the focal point for my driving ambition began suddenly to look pathetic and empty. What was the point in giving over my life to these things? The mask was being removed from my life.

I began to wonder, Did my old man tell this preacher about me? But no; I did not even know myself I would be listening to this until I stopped at the door. I was not converted that night, though I promised the preacher that I would come to the church again.

It was three weeks before I saw him. I was driving along beside the sea in the old lorry we used at the farm, when I spotted him walking beside the road, carrying a Calor gas cylinder. He had about a mile to go yet. I said to myself, 'Will I stop, or will I go roaring past him? If I give him a lift, he'll ask me why I haven't been back in church.' In the end I stopped, and said quite roughly to him, 'Want a lift, Jock?' He wanted a lift all right! He threw the cylinder in the back and climbed up beside me. Just as I thought, the first thing he said to me was, 'You never came back to church.'

'No—I've been busy.' 'You are a liar.'

'That's a terrible thing for a preacher to say.'

'But you are a liar. It wasn't because you were busy—am I right?'

'I suppose you are.'

He shouted above the sound of the old engine, 'You know what I think? I think you are running scared. I think you are scared that you will get converted.'

'No, I'm not scared. Actually, I would like to be converted, but I don't think I can be.'

'What do you mean?'

'Well, since that night, I have asked God two or three times to convert me and nothing has happened.'

By this time we had reached where he was staying. He said, 'Why don't you come in?'

It can't be as simple as that!

I went in with him, and he talked to me as no one had ever talked before. Then he said to me, 'If you are really serious about this, what about going down on your knees, and we will ask God to change you.'

I wasn't very keen. I was embarrassed, but then I said to myself, 'I want this if I can get it.' So I went down on my knees. At first he wanted me to pray, but there was no way I was going to do that with him there. I said, 'You are the one who is paid to do the praying. You pray!'

He began to talk to God as if he really knew him, and as he continued he quoted John 3:16: 'God so loved the world, that he gave his only begotten Son, that whosoever believeth in him should not perish, but have everlasting life.' I had known these words all my life, but as he quoted them it was as if someone drew aside curtains so that light came into a dark room. I understood these words in a new way. I saw that Christ had finished all that was necessary for my salvation. I didn't have to do anything to save my soul. I got a hold of the preacher's arm and said, 'Say that again!'

He stared at me. 'Say what again?'

'That bit about God loving the world. Say that again!' He repeated the text.

I said, 'Does that mean that if I really believe that Jesus is the Son of God, and that he died on the cross at Calvary to save us from our sins, and trust him because of that, I will be saved?'

He said, 'Yes—that's just what it means.' I said, 'It can't be as simple as that!'

But although I was arguing like that, I felt I was understanding the way of salvation for the first time in my life. What I had known, in one way, for so long, now seemed so new! And as I believed it for the first time, a great peace began to flood into my heart, and a stillness came over me.

Then I thought, 'That's all right, but you know how a Christian is supposed to live.' I began thinking of all the things I would have to stop. He saw my face changing and asked, 'What's wrong now?'

I said, 'I don't think I could live like a Christian. I would have to give up too much.'

'Listen, Douglas', he said. 'You think through everything you feel you would have to give up. Think about it very carefully.' Then he said, 'In this hand [holding out his right hand] I'll give you everything you are afraid of losing; and in this hand [holding out his left hand] I'll give you Christ.'

He didn't make it easy for me. I'm sure I must have sat there for ten minutes (he said afterwards it felt like an eternity), thinking deeply about all that was involved. Then at last I absolutely knew which one I had to take. I said, 'If I can really have Christ as my Saviour, I'll take him.' As soon as I had said that, my heart was filled with joy and love.

• Then I suddenly remembered my father. I had dropped him off in the village at two o'clock. He was going to collect his pension and visit a friend, and I was to have picked him up at four o'clock. By this time it was twenty past seven!

I said to the preacher, 'Man, I've forgotten my old man. He has been waiting on me for three and a half hours.' I jumped into the old lorry and went roaring off back to the little bungalow where my father had said he would be. The lady came to the door and let me in. I hurried ahead of her into the living room. My father was sitting opposite the door. As soon as I came in he got up, crossed the room, took me in his arms and said, 'Douglas, thank God.'

'Why?'

'You've been converted.' 'How do you know?'

'I could see in your face, as soon as you came in the door, that my prayer had been answered.'

25

Call to the ministry

By the time I had been a Christian for two years, I was quite sure that the Lord was calling me to preach the gospel. I tried to satisfy this demanding heart-urge by applying for, and getting, acceptance as, a Lay Preacher with my local Presbytery. Having spoken at one or two of the little weekly prayer meetings conducted by my father, I preached my first sermon in Lochgilphead Free Church in March 1957. My father died in June of that year, and it was in the days following that momentous—but in some ways marvellous—event that I knew I would have to seek entrance to the ministry of the gospel.

At the end of August 1958, I left home to take up full-time study at Skerry's College, Edinburgh, with a view to entering the ministry of the Free Church of Scotland. I had, of course, at least four years of secondary school studies to make up and knew that I was facing an uphill task. Over the next two years, my time was spent in studying for University Preliminary Entrance exams.

My only source of income, once I stopped work, was an annual grant of £70 from the church. So, to make ends meet, I drove a lorry in the afternoons for a haulier who used to camp on our farm over the summer holidays. He and his wife were tremendously kind to me at that time, and a great help during a period when I felt very homesick and missed my dogs, my sheep and my hills.

Throughout that period, though, the Lord was really good to me. I enjoyed listening to fine preaching, made many new Christian friends and, within two years, gained passes which enabled me to enter Aberdeen University. I enjoyed my time there enormously, marrying at the end of my first session, and graduating MA in 1963. I then returned to Edinburgh to pursue my theological studies at the Free Church College.

Places of service

I was ordained to the gospel ministry, and inducted to my first pastorate in St Columba Free Church, Aberdeen, on 3 September 1966. The congregation was not large, but both Mary and I knew it well from our student days, and over the last few years of my predecessor's very faithful ministry it had not only grown in numbers, but had increased in spiritual vigour as well, and there was a fine tone and quality to its life. We knew that during the university sessions there would be quite a number of students amongst us.

During my time in the Dee Street Church, as it was most popularly known, my ministry was quite varied, with a lot of hospital visiting, evangelism amongst lapsed churchgoers, openair meetings, street tracting, and work amongst college and university students. We saw the Lord at work amongst the people there, and over the years quite a number of young people were converted. This was one of the happiest periods of my life, and I enjoyed the work tremendously. I was quite heartbroken when I felt the time had come to leave for another church.

In 1974 I was given and, after much heart-searching, accepted a call to St. Vincent Street Free Church in Glasgow. The work there was different from Aberdeen, but I also enjoyed it a great deal. There I saw quite a number of older people being converted—indeed, the first person and the last whom I knew to be definitely converted to Christ there were both over seventy years of age, something which I always regarded as quite unusual. Anyway, I ministered very happily there until 1982, when I was appointed to the chair of Church History and Church Principles in the Free Church College, Edinburgh.

I had eight years at the College and much enjoyed working with the men studying for the ministry of our own and various other churches. I was able to speak and preach in many places outside Scotland, and came to know the Lord's work on a wider scale than formerly.

I had just indicated acceptance of a call to a congregation in Edinburgh, where I am now ministering, when I took ill with coronary disease in the late spring of 1990. That eventuated in open-heart surgery and a triple bypass in July of that year. It was my first-ever experience of hospital or of serious illness, and it is a great joy for me to say that through all this rather traumatic experience I was very deeply aware of the Saviour's presence, and felt my heart fortified by his peace.

I was very humbled by the large number of calls and letters we received—from all around the world, almost—assuring us of continued prayer both from churches and individuals. And those prayers were wonderfully answered. It was a marvellous experience to feel myself absolutely cushioned with the love and power of Christ on the evening before my operation, and not merely to know, but actually to feel, that I was on the receiving end of a huge battery of Christian love and Christian prayer.

Over the months since then, I have made steady progress back to health and have been able to pick up the beginnings of a new ministry amongst a people from whom, and in whom, I receive many tokens of the Lord's love and graciousness. On the medical side of things I have also received great kindness, as well as dedicated and attentive care. I have marvelled at the skill, patience and sheer professionalism of all the people involved in this ministry of healing and, under God, owe them a great deal.

Gratitude to God

I feel that I owe a special debt of gratitude to the Lord for the help and support I have had from my wife Mary in our thirty years together, as well as during this last year and its times of illness and utter weakness. As I have indicated, she is also a graduate of Aberdeen University, was a teacher prior to our marriage, and is the daughter of a well-known Free Church minister and writer, the late Revd Murdoch Campbell, Resolis. Mary has been a great help right through my ministry and has made our home a place where people feel welcome.

We have five children: Eilidh (Gaelic for Helen), Murdo, Mhairi (Mary), Neil and Douglas. All of them are grown up now and are deeply committed Christians. The first is a social worker in Inverness; the second works with the Department of Agriculture; the third is a clinical psychologist; the fourth is studying for the ministry of our church; and the youngest is a student in Cardiff.

Looking back over my life, the greatest thing which ever happened to me was, without a shadow of a doubt, my conversion in 1955. I have never regretted that the Lord sought and found me, a lost, unworthy sinner, and changed my heart and life with his grace and power. The Lord has been very gracious and good to me down through the years and has never failed me.

My only regrets lie along the line of my own many failures to be all that I should have been for him. But despite the sins and disobedience, and the imperfect service I have been able to give to the Lord, I would not want to change any of it. My life has been full and happy, and every day has been rich with his love and mercy.

I would like to guard against the thought that I am in any way special, or that my experience, although so uniquely personal, is any different in principle from that of other Christians. It is not so. I am a very ordinary person who was found and saved by a very extraordinary Saviour, and I owe him a debt that can never be repaid either in this world or in the world to come. The wonder that filled my heart the night I first found Jesus in June 1955 is still there—the complete wonder that, as Paul put it long ago, he 'loved me, and gave himself for me'.

The above testimony has been reprinted from *The God of All Grace* by kind permission of Christian Focus Publications Ltd.

II. Addresses on
Psalm 23

The Lord's my Shepherd, I'll not want:
   He makes me down to lie
In pastures green; He leadeth me
   The quiet waters by.

My soul He doth restore again,
   And me to walk doth make
Within the paths of righteousness,
   E'en for His own Name's sake.

Yea, though I walk through death's dark vale,
   Yet will I fear none ill;
For Thou art with me, and Thy rod
   And staff me comfort still.

My table Thou hast furnishèd
   In presence of my foes;
My head Thou dost with oil anoint,
   And my cup overflows.

Goodness and mercy all my life
   Shall surely follow me;
And in God's house for evermore
   My dwelling-place shall be.

Scottish Psalter, 1650

1

The 'Shepherd' theme

'The LORD is my shepherd'
(Psalm 23:1)

I have felt led of the Lord, I believe, to take as our theme for this conference one that we find very broadly scattered through Scripture. It is the 'Shepherd' theme—God as the Shepherd of his flock, and the Christian believers as the sheep of his flock. I would like to focus our studies in that theme, of course, on the twenty-third psalm. This psalm is the one that naturally comes to mind when we think of God as the Shepherd of his people, or of believers as his sheep. I am sure there are few portions of God's Word more familiar to every Christian believer. Six verses only, and yet I would guess that they are amongst the best-known verses of Scripture.

Now the very fact that we are focusing our thinking on the theme of 'God the Shepherd of his people', and on a portion of Scripture so familiar and so well-loved, constitutes, I think, a great difficulty for the preacher, and possibly for the hearer too; because, you see, you already know this psalm, and immediately a preacher announces that he is going to preach from it, you say, 'Well, what on earth can he say about Psalm 23 that I don't know already?' Let me say at the outset, I can say very little about Psalm 23 that you don't know already. I have to confess that.

So that is the difficulty. And I think there is a further difficulty for any preacher approaching a part of God's Word that is very well-loved, and that has already been owned and blessed of the Lord in most lives here present. Any preacher who is going to handle a portion of Scripture that God has made precious is very conscious that, in doing so, he may well bruise and hurt what is already precious.

Difficulties ... and helps

Now I realise all these dangers. I have been deeply conscious of them in preparing for this conference, and I think I have been conscious of them ever since I began preaching. I think I had been preaching for eighteen years before I ever went anywhere near Psalm 23 in a pulpit. I have been preaching for twenty-two years now, and I still wish that I could preach and tell people what I find in this psalm.

So I recognise the difficulty that the preacher faces in speaking from a passage like this. And I recognise your difficulties too. You don't want to have your precious things taken out and handled by a rough, rude fellow from Scotland, and some of your most cherished ideas perhaps knocked a little bit askew.

But if there are difficulties, then I think too that there are helps. I think, for example, that although I am a stranger to most of you, the very fact that I am handling and dealing with something that you are familiar with will help you to relax. And you will concentrate, I hope, not on the man who is preaching, but upon what the man is saying. So that's a help.

Then, you see, if you know not only the psalm but the Shepherd of the psalm, that gives me a real link with you, doesn't it? And that makes it much easier. It means that I can relax when I am preaching too—and if there is one thing I hate, it is trying to preach when I am tense and nervous! So I hope that the Lord, as we gather around this very familiar part of the Word, will allow you to relax and to look at himself, and allow me to relax as I try and lead our thoughts.

A widespread theme

Now, as I have said, the 'Shepherd' theme is very widely spread right through the Scriptures. It is not only in Psalm 23 that we find that God has been so gracious and has stooped so low in his mercy that he allows himself, the High and Holy One of Israel, to be compared to a shepherd with his sheep. We find it away back in Genesis.

We find, for example, Jacob referring to God as his shepherd when he is praying a blessing on the children of Joseph, Manasseh and Ephraim. In Genesis 48 we read: 'Jacob blessed Joseph and said, God, before whom my fathers Abraham and Isaac did walk, the God which fed me all my life long unto this day, the Angel which redeemed me from all evil, bless the lads' (verses 15,16).

Now I want you to notice one word there—'the God which *fed* me all my life'. The word there in the original Hebrew is the very same as the word translated 'shepherd' in Psalm 23, because the word 'shepherd' in Hebrew is just a participle of the verb that means 'to feed'. You see, this is the central task of a shepherd, to feed his sheep. Away back there, as he was praying God's blessing upon his children's children, Jacob wanted nothing more for them than that they should know the God that had shepherded him, and the God who, through the Angel of his Covenant, had delivered him from evil.

Then, of course, you find this theme right through the psalms— Psalms 74, 78, 80, and many others too numerous to mention. In Isaiah, Jeremiah and Ezekiel, too, you find God under the emblem of a shepherd, and again and again through the Minor Prophets you find Scripture speaking of God's people as God's flock, the people of his pasture, his sheep.

So it is a very widespread theme through Scripture, and a theme that, ever since I came to know Christ, has been particularly close to my own heart—perhaps for no other reason than that the first twelve years of my working life—from the age of thirteen and a half until I was twenty-five—were spent shepherding in the hills of North Argyllshire. When I came to know the Lord, I think he drew me to that theme in Scripture, and I was able to interpret much of the Lord's dealings with myself from my own experience among sheep. So, you see, it is a shepherd that is talking to you and not a preacher; and I hope you will put up with a shepherd!

Knowing the Shepherd

As we look at the psalm, the first thing we see about it is this, that David the psalmist knows God as his own Shepherd: 'The LORD is *my* shepherd'. The psalm begins with a strong note of personal assurance.

It is a great thing to have personal assurance in the Christian life. Now that personal assurance of David's is not ill-founded: he knows the Shepherd, and he *knows* that he knows him. That is where the Christian's assurance rests—not only in the fact of knowing that we are redeemed by the precious blood of Christ, but in the fact that we *know* we know. I say that because I believe it is possible for grace to come into a life, and for that life to go on without always knowing it for certain. I have met people who seem to lack Christian assurance, and yet I and others see the grace and the work of God's Spirit in them. They know the Saviour, but they don't always know that they know him. It is a great blessing not merely to know the Saviour but to know that you know him, so that you can say, 'The LORD is *my* shepherd'. Now I want to stress this at the very beginning, because this psalm really has nothing to do with you if you don't know the Shepherd of whom the psalm speaks. One of the saddest things in my life as a minister is this. I have to attend many funerals and, very frequently, funerals of people who know nothing about the Shepherd. And inevitably in Scotland they want us to sing

Psalm 23. There are godless people at funerals who will sing 'The Lord's my Shepherd', and in the ugly presence of death and the solemn reality of eternity they will take comfort from this that does not belong to them. Over the last two or three years I have frequently refused the request to sing Psalm 23 at the funerals of unbelieving men and women, because they have got nothing to do with the Shepherd and the blessings that this psalm enumerates.

Let me say very bluntly, at the beginning of our conference talks, that if you are here at this conference and you do not know this Shepherd, if you cannot say with David in a real personal way, 'The Lord Jehovah is *my Shepherd*', then a great deal of what I am saying does not and cannot apply to you. I would urge you to come to know the Shepherd of the psalm rather than just the psalm itself, because if you come to know the Shepherd, then you will come to know the psalm.

The wider setting

Now I want us to begin not with an exposition of the psalm, but to do something else. Psalm 23 is not an isolated unit. One of the first lessons that I and all the preachers here present were taught about preaching was this: never isolate your text from the context. One of the great dangers in preaching is that we do this. We pluck words out of their setting in God's Word and then pour our own ideas into them. That is how sects and 'isms' and heresies flourish—by isolating texts from God's Word. Now that is true not just of a text or a verse, but it is true of chapters of God's Word, and it is true of whole books of God's Word. It is good for us to know the background, the historical setting, and so on.

Psalm 23 is not in isolation: it is part, for example, of the Book of Psalms; and the Book of Psalms (and we generalise) deals particularly with Christian experience. The whole of the Psalter deals with Christian experience; sometimes it deals with very happy Christian experience, sometimes with very dark Christian experience—as, for example, 'Lord, from the depths to thee I cry' (Psalm 130). But it is a book which speaks particularly to God's people; it belongs to God's people.

Psalm 23, then, has to be related to the rest of the Book of Psalms. But it has to be related to something else too, for the Book of Psalms is only a part of a wider whole. So, you see, we have to let the light of the rest of Scripture shine on this particular passage.

Who is the Shepherd of Psalm 23?

Now, keeping that in mind, I want us to ask two questions. The first question, and one that is fundamental to our understanding of what the psalm is about, is, Who is the Shepherd of whom Psalm 23 speaks?

'Well,' you say, 'that's very easy. I know my Hebrew well enough after listening to those learned men in the pulpit. Psalm 23 begins with "Jehovah is my Shepherd".'

That is absolutely right. But who is Jehovah? Well, Jehovah is especially the covenant name of the Creator God, of the Triune God, Father, Son and Holy Spirit, and it is the name that speaks of God in relation to men as sinners. Further, it speaks of God in relation to men who are sinners but who have come under his saving purpose, his covenant of grace.

Away back there in Genesis, when Jacob was seeking a blessing for his children's children, he was looking to the God who had made and kept covenant with him, to Jehovah who had fed and shepherded him, and who had especially revealed himself to him as the Angel, the Messenger of the Covenant. Now we cannot doubt who that Messenger was. I don't think we can even doubt the incident Jacob had in mind.

Do you remember when Jacob, after being away from his home for twenty years, was coming back with his two wives, their children, and a whole herd of animals? He was, he thought, threatened by Esau, and he spent the night wrestling with the Angel of God. God laid hold of Jacob and Jacob laid hold of God, and Jacob was blessed. Although I don't believe that was his conversion experience, I do think that his life had a new quality about it from that moment. He was humbled, and he was always more dependent on God after that.

The Angel who delivered him from evil was Christ, the Messenger or the Angel of the Covenant, in what one would call a pre-incarnation appearance. So this 'Shepherd' theme deals with God who is the God of the covenant of grace, and it deals, specifically, with God in his saving relationship to his people. When God reveals himself in a saving relationship, it is always through the Angel of the Covenant.

Now time will not allow me to take you through all the relevant passages in the Old Testament, but let us do something that we frequently have to do. Let us go to the New Testament and let the New Testament throw its light back on the teachings of the Old Testament. When we go to the New Testament, taking with us our question, Who is the Shepherd of Psalm 23?, we find, I think, wonderfully clear light on who that Shepherd really is. I want to go to just three places in the New Testament that point to Jesus as the Shepherd of God's sheep—and, therefore, the Shepherd of Psalm 23—and they are all places that will be familiar to you.

The Good Shepherd

The first is John 10:11. There Jesus was talking to people, let us remember, who were steeped in Old Testament Scripture; people who knew that Jehovah was their Shepherd, and that he was *their* Shepherd as he was the Shepherd of no other people. Jesus stood before these people, and this is what he said: 'I am the good shepherd: the good shepherd giveth his life for the sheep.'

I want you to notice two things about that claim of Jesus. First of all, simply this: Jesus is identifying himself with the Shepherd of Old Testament Scripture—'I am the good shepherd'. To the Jewish person that meant only one thing: it meant God. There was only one good; there was only one Shepherd; there was only one who had the right to the title 'The Good Shepherd'. Here is someone they knew, someone who was brought up amongst them, and he stands out in front of them and says, 'I am the good shepherd'. If you go down to the thirty-third verse in that chapter, you will find that they charge him with blasphemy. Why? Because he made himself to be equal with God. You see, that is what his claim was—'I am the good shepherd'. It was a claim to full and absolute deity, to identity with the one they knew as the Good Shepherd. Make no mistake about it: Jesus of Nazareth claimed absolute identity with God, the eternal one.

Don't listen to the preachers who will tell you today that Jesus never claimed to be divine! Of course he did! Just read John 10, and you will find that not only did he make the claim, but he was understood to make it. He made it unmistakably: 'I am the good shepherd.'

Then Jesus went on to indicate what the leading characteristic of the Good Shepherd is: 'I am the good shepherd: the good shepherd giveth his life for the sheep.' There is the main characteristic of Jesus as the Good Shepherd—he 'giveth his life for the sheep'. Notice that he does not say that the Good Shepherd dies for his sheep. That is a truth, and it is a wonderful truth, but it is not the truth that Jesus teaches here. The truth that he is teaching here is far more wonderful: He is saying that the Good Shepherd comes to give a voluntary sacrifice of himself. In verses 17 and 18 he says that he 'lays down' his life. It is not that his life is to be wrested from him, but he is to give it freely, voluntarily.

He goes on to give the authority that he had for laying down his life: 'This commandment have I received of my Father' (verse

18), and 'Therefore doth my Father love me, because I lay down my life' (verse 17). He relates his messianic and his priestly activity to the will of God the Father. Now that is important. He is not doing something that he has set out to do on his own; he is fulfilling a commission that was given him by his Father. Suicide is sin. This man is without sin, and he has to be without sin even in his sacrificial giving of himself into death. He has the authority (as the word could better be translated) of the fountain and source of life, his Father, to do that: 'This commandment have I received of my Father.'

You see, the difference between the sacrificial death of Jesus and the death of every other man is that he himself is active in it. What a stress the Pauline epistles put on that! For you, for me, for every one of us, when death comes we will be victims. But this was not so for Jesus. When death came to Jesus of Nazareth, our Lord, he was not its victim, he was its conqueror. He took death to himself: 'Into thy hands I commend my spirit.'

I once heard Professor John Murray put it like this: 'Death was not his fate, it was his deed.' Death was his triumphal act, and he was never more active in all his ministry than he was in the act of death. What was he doing? In the words of Professor Murray: 'It is as though the eternal Son of God took his human body in one hand and his human soul in the other, and he rent them, rent them apart.' That is what death was for Jesus, as it is for us—the separation of soul from body. And the separation of his soul from his body was his own act, the personal act of the eternal Son of God.

Let us never forget that. Here is the Shepherd laying down his life for the sheep, giving himself unto death. And, you know, there is something very wonderful there. Death was vanquished and quenched by Jesus, because this is what happened. It is as though with one of those divine hands he holds his body in the grave, and with the other he holds his soul in his Father's presence—and, you see, they are united still. He lives still in his eternal sonship. So body and soul are still linked to him; they are not really sundered; they are still held, and they are held in union. Death has severed one bond, and when it has severed one bond it has run into another bond—that bond which links his human nature, body and soul, to his divine person. And when that link was forged, when he took a human nature to himself, it was forged as a link that was never to be broken.

This is one of the wonders of the incarnation of the Son of God, that he took human nature, which will be his for all eternity, and he took it in order to lay down his life, in order that death could come into his experience—he who was the eternal Son of God! How does Hebrews 9 put it? 'Who through the eternal Spirit offered himself without spot to God' (verse 14). Here it is; here is the Good Shepherd laying down his life for the sheep.

The Good Shepherd, then, is to be identified with Jesus of Nazareth. He made that identification himself. Jesus of Nazareth, therefore, is to be identified with the God of the Covenant. His leading characteristic as the Good Shepherd is this, that he gives his life, he lays it down, a sacrifice for the sheep.

The Great Shepherd
Now we come to another very familiar portion of the New Testament, the Epistle to the Hebrews, and we get still more light here on our question, Who is the Shepherd of Psalm 23? In Hebrews 13:20, Paul—I believe it is Paul; some don't—is closing a letter which has been written especially to Jewish believers, to Hebrews. It was written to believers who were afraid that when they lost all the sparkle and glitter and attractiveness of the Mosaic ritual and its ceremonies, they had lost many great privileges. One of the basic concerns of this letter is to tell them that they have not suffered loss; they have gained realities, and types and shadows have fled.

The letter closes with a prayer for them. This is one of the great Pauline benedictions, I believe, and it is a wonderful one, isn't it? 'Now the God of peace'—what a lovely title! But why can Paul talk about God, the holy and awful (or terrible) one, as 'the God of peace'? For the very simple reason that he made peace. How did he make peace? He made peace through the Good Shepherd who laid down his life, or, as Paul says in this prayer, 'through the blood of the everlasting covenant' (Hebrews 13:20). God has been reconciled; God can now be known as 'the God of peace'. Let me ask you this. Do you know God, and know him as the God of peace, who brings peace into your heart, and who allows you to live in all the turmoil of this awful world with his peace undergirding you and holding you and keeping you calm? He is 'the God of peace'.

Now what is it that Paul is attributing specifically to the God of peace in this great benediction? The raising of Jesus from the dead. 'Now the God of peace, that brought again from the dead'—who else but God could do it?—'our Lord Jesus, that great shepherd of the sheep ...' Here again, you see, our Lord Jesus is identified for us clearly, unmistakably, as the Shepherd of the sheep. He is the 'great shepherd'. And do you see, now, what the leading characteristic of the Shepherd Jesus is here? As the Good Shepherd, his chief characteristic was that he laid down his life for the sheep. And now, as the Great Shepherd of the sheep, the leading characteristic of his shepherding is this—he has taken that life again. He has risen from the dead. Death could not hold him. Body and soul have been united again, you see. That is why he is able to shepherd: he is living.

One cannot spend much time on this, but it is put very simply for us in this same epistle. He is 'able to save'. Why? Because he 'ever lives to make intercession for us'. His death was absolutely necessary, but let us remember this: it is not only because of his death but also because of his life that he is able. He has been equipped to save because he ever lives. You see, he lives in 'the power of an endless life' (Hebrews 7:16). He lives in the power of a life that has been through the darkness and the fire of death; he lives in a life that could not be quenched. No wonder John Owen could write a book on the atonement and entitle it *The Death of Death in the Death of Christ.* Jesus, the Great Shepherd, lives.

You see, a dead shepherd is no use to a flock, is he? Just recently, my wife and family were down in London, and we were being shown over a church, at the end of which was a big cross, and on it a very ugly portraiture of the suffering Saviour. Our children were really horrified (they are Free Church, and very Presbyterian!). 'Daddy, look at that!', they said, 'Isn't that awful?' 'Well,' I asked, 'why is it awful?' And our youngest one, who is nine, said, 'Well, he's not dead now, is he?' Well, he is not dead; we serve a living Saviour.

The Chief Shepherd

We come now to the third place in the New Testament that will cast light on our question. In 1 Peter 5:4 we read, 'And when the chief Shepherd shall appear, ye shall receive a crown of glory that fadeth not away.'

Now Peter was writing specifically to people who were going to suffer persecution. 'Think it not strange', he said, 'concerning the fiery trial which is to try you' (1 Peter 4:12). What he is saying is this: 'Don't think it queer when a lot of fiery persecution meets you. Your faith has to be tested, and God is in control of all.' The essence of his message in this letter is, 'Be faithful.' Then, he says, if you are faithful, this is what happens: 'when the chief Shepherd shall appear, ye shall receive a crown of glory'. Here is Jesus again, and Jesus as the Chief Shepherd; and the leading characteristic of our Lord as the Chief Shepherd is to give 'a crown of glory'.

Now if you ask me what that means, I have to say this: I wish I knew. The New Testament talks about life and about glory; and then it talks about a crown of life and a crown of glory. Whatever it means, it must surely mean this, that at the second coming of Christ, and at the fulfilment of all things, there will be a completeness and a perfection of glory for every one of his people. And what will be the essence of that crown of glory? It will be this: we shall be like him.

This is what the apostle John says: 'it doth not yet appear what we shall be: but we know that, when he shall appear'—the same word and the same tense as in 1 Peter 5:4—'we shall be like him' (1 John 3:2). And then he says a very strange thing— 'for we shall see him as he is'. You see, that is why we shall be like him, because when we see him, his image is reflected in us, and thus we are made partakers of his glory. I think that is something to do with the crown of glory that Jesus gives us as the Chief Shepherd.

And, you see, the Chief Shepherd goes into the eternal realm. I suppose that something of the Good Shepherd is there too, because I believe he still bears the marks of his suffering (or we should call them, more properly, the marks of his *offering*, because he not only suffered, he offered). I would guess that something of the Great Shepherd, the resurrection-glory of our Lord Jesus Christ, will be seen too. But he will be, supremely, the Chief Shepherd. He is the one who will lead us 'unto living fountains of water' (Revelation 7:17). He will feed us—and he will feed us (strangely) as the *Lamb*! Well, who more fitted to know what a sheep needs than a lamb, because a lamb *is a* sheep?

You see, this is one of the wonders of the gospel, that our Shepherd—the Good Shepherd who laid down his life for us, the Great Shepherd who took it again, and the Chief Shepherd who will give a crown of glory—he is one with us. He is able to *sympathise* with us because he was tempted in all points, tested and tried like as we are. We have a perfect, sympathetic, wonderful Shepherd in our Lord Jesus.

Now come back to Psalm 23. We have been asking the question, Who is the Shepherd of Psalm 23? The Old Testament tells us that it was Jehovah, and the New Testament tells us that it was Jehovah–Jesus, the Good Shepherd, the Great Shepherd, the Chief Shepherd of the flock of God. In answering that question we have been setting Psalm 23 against a wider background, and specifically against the clear teaching of the New Testament. And I think we need that background.

What is the setting of Psalm 23?

But now I want to come closer still to the psalm and ask another question: What is the setting of Psalm 23? What do I mean by that? Well, where in your Bible do you find Psalm 23? You say, 'Well, preacher, that's very easy. Psalm 23 comes after Psalm 22.' That is absolutely right. But now I want to ask you another question: What is Psalm 22? Well, listen to it! Listen to its opening words: 'My God, my God, why hast thou forsaken me?' Where are we when we enter into Psalm 22? We are at a place called Calvary.

Go through this psalm, and you are closer to Calvary than any of the Gospels can take you, because you are not merely looking at the one who is offering his life, but you are in his mind and you are in his heart. You are sharing and seeing his suffering, in a way that the history of the Gospels cannot allow you to see and share his suffering. You are listening to his heartbeat as he says,

they … laugh me to scorn … saying, He trusted on the LORD … let him deliver him … strong bulls of Bashan have beset me round [Bashan was famous for its breeding bulls—

strong, terrifying animals] ... I am poured out like water ... they pierced my hands and my feet.

Where are we? We are at a place called Calvary, and we are seeing the Good Shepherd laying down his life for the sheep. We are seeing what it cost for Jesus to suffer and to offer. We are seeing what it cost this Shepherd (if I can put it like that) to get into Psalm 23. There was only one gateway for the Son of God to become the Shepherd of the sheep, and that was by the gateway of Psalm 22 and his suffering on the cross.

Let me say this—I say it with all reverence, but I make absolutely no apology for saying it. Even God could never have written Psalm 23 and its opening words, until there had first of all been the divine purpose to bring about the events of which Psalm 22 speaks. He will deal with sinners only on the basis of blood and only on the basis of sacrifice. We have to say this, you see, that even for God to get into Psalm 23 there had to come Psalm 22 in the experience of the Son of God.

The cross

Much more so, my friend, before you and I can get into Psalm 23, we have to go by the pathway of Psalm 22. There is only one gateway into the flock of the Lord Jesus Christ, and that gateway stands by the cross. That is why this psalm does not belong to any but those who come by way of the cross. It is only when you have been broken and humbled at the feet of Jesus the Good Shepherd, who has laid down his life for you, that you really become one of his sheep. There is no other way.

Knowing your Bible, that is good, but it will not save your soul. Going to church or chapel, that is good, but it is not salvation. Saying 'The LORD is my shepherd', that is good too, but it can be nothing but a lie unless you come through Psalm 22 and have seen your God in Christ crucified for your sin.

The throne

Let me ask you the question again: Where is Psalm 23? You say, 'Well, it's after Psalm 22, and it's just before Psalm 24.' And you are absolutely right. What is Psalm 24? Well, just listen to it: 'Who shall ascend into the hill of the LORD? ... He that hath clean hands, and a pure heart'.

There was only one pair of clean hands in this world, and men took them and drove nails through their palms. 'He that hath clean hands, and a pure heart'—he shall ascend. And has he? Yes! Just listen!

Ye gates, lift up your heads on high;
Ye doors that last for aye,
Be lifted up ...

Why? Because the Shepherd who laid down his life and who took it again is entering into a throne. Where is the Shepherd of God and the Shepherd of God's people today? He has ascended on high, and he has led captivity captive, says the psalmist (Psalm 68). He has made a mockery of the triumph of his enemies, and he is exalted in the midst of the throne.

You see, the three psalms are linked together. In Psalm 22 you find a depiction of the Good Shepherd laying down his life for the sheep. In Psalm 23 you find the Great Shepherd who has taken his life again, and who lovingly will shepherd and pasture every one of his sheep and lead them from a knowledge of himself, or in a knowledge of himself, to the Father's house for evermore. And then in Psalm 24 you have the glory of the Chief Shepherd, the one who is ascended into glory in order to give glory to his sheep, to make them like himself.

I once heard Professor Finlayson preaching on Psalm 23, and he linked Psalms 22 to 24 like this: 'One is the psalm of the cross, the next is the psalm of the crook, and the third is the psalm of the crown.' They stand together, and each of them sheds its own particular light upon the Shepherd who is our Shepherd, our Lord Jesus Christ. And these lights blend, and they light up his glory, and they show him to be a Great Shepherd.

'The LORD is my shepherd.' Is this Lord *your* Shepherd? My friend, let me say this. If this Lord is your Shepherd, you have not yet begun to know how blessed you are, how God has blessed you. And if this Lord is not your Shepherd, you have not yet begun to know how poor and how miserable and how blind and how naked you really are before your God and your Creator.

2

A living relationship

'My sheep hear my voice, and I know them,
and they follow me'—(John 10:27)

We have been attempting to look at the twenty-third psalm from a wider viewpoint by finding the answer to the questions, Who is the Shepherd of Psalm 23? and What is the setting of Psalm 23? Now I hope you are not expecting me to go straight into an exposition of the psalm, because if you are you are going to be disappointed! I want us to stand back from it a little still, before we come to an actual attempt at exposition of its truths.

Specifically at this point I want us to ask another two simple questions. Although they are very simple questions, they are absolutely crucial, I think, to an understanding of what Psalm 23 is really about. The first one is, Who are the sheep that are involved in Psalm 23? and the second, What kind of sphere are we moving in? what kind of sphere of life does Psalm 23 hold out to us?

These two questions are very closely related, and in fact we shall take them back to front. We shall take the second question first, because if we look at the sphere in which Psalm 23 moves we shall be finding our answer to who the sheep of Psalm 23 are. Who, then, are the sheep? And what kind of relationship, what kind of life, what life-view is held out to us in the twenty-third psalm?

Come back to the psalm for just a moment, and to its opening words, 'The LORD is my shepherd'. As I have said already, this is really the important thing about Psalm 23—that we be able to say truly and factually, 'The LORD is *my* shepherd.' To know the psalm is not enough. Fundamental to the whole outlook of the psalm and the sphere in which it breathes and moves is to know not just the psalm but the Shepherd; to be able to say that he is *my Shepherd.* It is the psalm of the staff or the shepherding; that is its sphere, the sphere in which it is ordered, its atmosphere.

Its gateway

Now it has become that, as we have seen, because Psalm 22 is 'the psalm of the sword'. In it we have the fulfilment of the prophecy in Zechariah: 'Awake, O sword, against my shepherd, and against the man that is my fellow ... smite the shepherd.' We see God's sword smiting the Shepherd in Psalm 22.

But that psalm is not merely a depicting of Calvary, of the great event that took place when the Good Shepherd laid down his life for the sheep. It goes on to tell us what the laying down of the life of the Shepherd leads to. Calvary is not merely an event. The death of the Lord Jesus on the cross is more than an act; it is a declaration of God. The cross is not just historical reality, though it is that; it is a message from God. It is the very central message of God's good news to man.

The declaration

What does the cross say? Well, go back for a second to Psalm 22, verse 22. The one who has been suffering, the one who has been in anguish, says this: 'I will declare thy name unto my brethren'. His declaring of the name of the God under whom he is suffering all the things that the psalm speaks about is not something separate from his sufferings; it is something involved in his sufferings. Do you remember how Paul puts it? 'God commends

52

[placards] his love to us ...' How does he do that? He manifests, advertises, commends his love to us, 'in that, while we were yet sinners, Christ died for us.'

The cross is itself the most powerful declaration of God's grace and love to sinners. It is the heart of God's message to you as one who is lost—and to me. The fact that it is more than an event—that its message and declaration are ultimate proof of God's love—makes it the gateway into the sphere, the atmosphere, of Psalm 23. It is that declaration which brings a lost sinner to be a sheep, and ushers him into the order in which Psalm 23 moves and lives, and in which the person in Psalm 23 has his being.

A New Testament floodlight

Now I want us to try and do something similar to what we have done already—to allow the light of the New Testament to shine back on to this great truth of the psalm and its gateway. When we go in at the gate of the psalm we are coming into the atmosphere of the psalm and we are answering these two questions (we cannot really separate them): What is the sphere of the psalm? And who are the sheep of whom Psalm 23 talks?

I want you to come with me to John 10, and we shall isolate one very brief verse there and use it as a floodlight back on the truths that are occupying our minds. Jesus said these words: 'My sheep hear my voice, and I know them, and they follow me' (John 10:27).

Relationship

Now the opening statement of Psalm 23, 'The LORD is my shepherd', is the foundation of the whole psalm, the thing on which everything else is built. And this foundation speaks about relationship—'The LORD is *my* shepherd.' If the Lord is my Shepherd, then that means that I am his sheep.

I want to pause here for just a moment and say a very simple and yet, I think, a very important thing. It is sheep, and the possession of sheep, that makes a shepherd. Were there no sinners, the eternal Son of God would never have had the glory that is his as a Saviour–Redeemer. What a wonderful thing God has done over against the malignant movement of sin and evil! God has purposed to save, and isn't it wonderful that a holy and righteous God will save?

The Saviour's glory

But it is more wonderful still, because he has purposed not only to save, but to save in a way which will magnify the name of his Son for the endless ages of eternity! God, in the person of his Son incarnate, has not only become a Saviour, my dear friends, but a Saviour who can save you in a way that will glorify his triune name. Isn't that wonderful? For if his Son had had no sheep, he would have been no Shepherd. Were there no sinners, there would be no need of a Saviour.

But he *is* a Shepherd; he is *my* Shepherd. Possession. I possess him: that is a wonderful truth, to know that you are saved and that your soul is redeemed. But there is a more wonderful truth, and it is this: not only to know that I have a Saviour, but to know that my Saviour has me. That is what is involved, you see—a relationship; and a relationship is always two-sided.

Imagine, those of you who have husbands or wives or a girlfriend or a boy-friend. You say, 'I am having a relationship.' Well, it is a wonderful relationship where there is real love, but you cannot have a relationship like that if there is not another person, can you? There are two sides to every relationship.

Where you see a shepherd, you automatically look for his sheep; and where you see sheep, you think about the shepherd. I never drive along a road where I see sheep in the fields or on the mountain but I automatically think of the shepherd. I say to myself, 'I wonder what sort of guy is looking after these sheep.' That is natural to me, because for twelve years of my life I was looking after sheep.

In the same way, when you see a Christian, what do you think? Do you not think of the Saviour? Do you not think of the relationship that has two sides, both of which are required to make a whole? This is what Jesus is pointing out here in John 10:27—'My sheep hear my voice, and I know them, and they follow me.'

Talking to people

As we come closer to these words, let us remember that Jesus was talking to people who were steeped in the Old Testament Scriptures. He was talking to people who identified Jehovah God with themselves. He, the eternal Creator God, was their Shepherd. They knew Psalm 23, and they also knew Psalms 22 and 24. As Jesus was talking to them, you see how wonderfully he laid hold of their religious knowledge, their biblical background.

But he did something else. He laid hold of their everyday experience. For these folk were not only steeped in the Old Testament, but they were a pastoral people. Probably the vast majority of those who were listening to him owned sheep. So he was laying hold not only of their biblical knowledge but of their practical everyday experience to light up religious knowledge. Isn't it wonderful when you get a preacher who does that? Jesus was doing it constantly—relating undying eternal truths to everyday experience, bringing God to where people were.

Who am I to criticise preaching? But when I have to listen to preachers (and sometimes I do), I often feel, 'Well, that man is certainly preaching a great sermon. It would be a great sermon for people who lived a hundred years ago, and who were steeped in the Scriptures or in the Puritan tradition; but it doesn't mean much to the ignorance and the darkness of our day.' Very often the illustrations used from the pulpit date back two or three hundred years, don't they? No wonder people come out and say, 'No, I don't know what the man was talking about.' Well, why do we get into the pulpit at all if we let people go out thinking, 'I don't know what he was talking about'? Jesus didn't do that. He took hold of everyday experience.

Now I am talking to preachers especially. Don't try and shape great sermons. Try to preach and bring God to people. Forget yourself and forget how you are saying the thing. It is a terrible temptation, isn't it, when you know you have got to go and face people and you want to show them how good you are. You want to show them how you can use English and how well you know your Bible, and how much of the Puritans you have read—and you've read Berkhof as well! People don't, primarily, need to know that you have read Berkhof; they need to know that you are living with Jesus Christ, that Jesus Christ is important for you, and that he is important for them.

Now I am not decrying preparation. Of course you have to prepare, and of course you have to read and understand the Bible, and of course you want to use every tool that will aid you in your preaching. But get a hold of the people, no matter how you do it. I remember Willie Still in Aberdeen saying to me when I was a very young minister—and he was a man who had proved his own ministry—'Douglas, if I could get them to listen to me by swinging from the rafters, I would do it.' But I don't think he ever had to swing from the rafters!

Jesus laid hold of two branches of knowledge which are with many of us still, only one branch has become very slim. We can no longer take it for granted that people are steeped in the Word of God; they are not. But people still live in the same kind of world as their preacher does. Maybe they are not surrounded by sheep, but they are still surrounded by identifiable objects and tangible things. Lay hold of them, and use them to illustrate truth.

So here Jesus illustrates this relationship from two points of view. First of all, he illustrates it from the Shepherd's viewpoint. Two things are true of the Shepherd as he looks out at the sheep: they are 'My sheep ... and I know them'. Then he illustrates the relationship from the other side, the side of the sheep, and he makes two statements about this relationship: they 'hear my voice ... and they follow me'.

The Shepherd's viewpoint

Now let us look at the statements he makes—two twofold statements. We will look first at the relationship from the Shepherd's point of view. How does the Shepherd of Psalm 23 identify his sheep? Well, he does it in this twofold way. He says first of all that they are 'my sheep', and then he says, 'I know them'. Both are very important things, lovely things. Let us look at the first one first of all.

'My sheep'

What right does Jehovah–Jesus have to say of any other person, '*my* sheep'? In saying 'They are mine', he is touching personality; he is touching the dignity of individuality. What right does he have to make that kind of statement?

It is a statement, you see, that cuts across all that sin really is. Sin, in essence, is the assertion of autonomy by man. It is the denial of the sovereignty and the lordship of the Creator over us. And Jesus says that in this relationship this sovereignty is restored: they are '*my* sheep'.

Everyone who wants to live a Christian life has to face this. You are no longer going to be your own man or your own woman, or your own boy or girl. You are going to belong—every bit of you—to someone else. You are going to be a sheep who has a Shepherd. And it is time that Christians began to realise that. You are either *for Christ* and altogether his, or you have nothing to do with him. Jesus does not soften that down in any way. He says, 'Whosoever doth not bear his cross, and come after me, cannot be my disciple' (Luke 14:27).

'Well,' you say, 'what right does he have to claim such an ownership over me? We are important people.' No, we are lost sinners. We need him; he does not need us. He has a threefold right to make this assertion, '*my* sheep'—and it is a wonderful assertion!

Let us pause there for a moment. I would guess that anyone who has done much shepherding would always be fond of sheep. If he were not, he would never have been a shepherd in the first place, or he would not have stuck with it for long. Sheep are not the easiest creatures to be fond of. But a man who is shepherding his own sheep, who can expend all his work and time and energy on animals which he can say are 'mine', will give himself to the utmost.

It is a very wonderful thing that Jesus is saying here—'*my* sheep'. He is emphasising a truth which the New Testament tells us again and again. A verse that struck me in January or February this year, when I was reading (of all places) in Deuteronomy, was, 'The LORD's portion is his people' (32:9). They are his possession, his dearest gift; he prizes them. I wish that would strike us afresh. According to Scripture, the Lord's greatest possession, the thing that most interests him, is his people. Well, he gave his Son for them.

Gifted by his Father

The first reason why Jesus has the right to call us his is because every one of whom he says 'mine' was *gifted to* him by his Father. Now I don't need to make any apology for the Scriptures.

I would not do so even if you were all the greatest Arminians in the world! We make no apology for what God says. And this is what God says through his apostle: 'he hath chosen us in him before the foundation of the world' (Ephesians 1:4). Here we have the mystery of God's electing love.

But I want you to notice something that is often missed out. At the very centre of God's electing, choosing and predestinating of a people, was his love to his Son. Christ is the focal point of God's electing grace, because when he elected you to eternal salvation he elected you to salvation in Christ, and he elected Christ to the suffering and the offering of the cross. Election is not something hard and arbitrary that should make us afraid of a fearful God. It is something that should draw us into the very centre of God's wonderful, gracious love to lost sinners, because it focuses and centres in Christ.

What a gift! A multitude of lost sinners, that no man can number, given to his own Son! What a reception that gift received, because it was from the Father! We don't know why God chose to save sinners. He could have passed them by, and there would have been no spot on his glory. None deserved salvation. The only answer the Bible gives is this: he did it 'according to the good pleasure of his will' (Ephesians 1:5). Perhaps on this question we will be groping even in eternity, but I think that the answer lies in the relationship within the Trinity, and particularly in the love that the Father bore to the Son and the love that the Son bore to the Father. That love had to spill over, and it did; and it spilled over to unworthy objects.

Now, you see, if you get something as a gift from someone whom you love and who you believe loves you, you don't look at the gift and say, 'Well, dear me! Not much here, is there?' You look at the gift, even if it is very small, and you say, 'Well, what a time he must have spent getting this for me! Poor soul, he spent his last ten pence! But he did it because he loved me.'

I have quite a few Bibles in my study. One is very old, tattered and torn, and yet I never throw it out. Why? Not because I have any strange, superstitious misgivings about putting out old Bibles; but I hold on to this one because it was a gift to me by my father. He gave it to me two days after I was converted.

I was converted on 14 June 1955, and I knew that my father had been praying for me for years before that. I used to get up in the spring at half-past three in the morning (sometimes it was half-past two) and be off to the hills. My father was getting old then, and deaf, and he slept downstairs at the back, near the door where I had to go out. When I was going to the hills (sometimes after nights that I would not talk about now), I would hear my father praying, and I would hear him mentioning before God his six children. I knew that my father was praying for me. On 16 June, two days after I was converted, he gave me a copy of the Bible, on which he had inscribed, 'From a father who loves, and who prays because he loves.' You see, that Bible is precious to me because in it I see the love of my father to me.

I believe that every one of his people is precious to Christ because they were the gift of the Father to him. He looks on you, and he doesn't feel what you feel. You feel so unworthy and so unlovely. You are just a tattered kind of gift, aren't you? But what does the Lord Jesus see when he looks at you? He sees his Father's love to himself. They are his by gift—'those that thou gavest me, I have kept' (John 17:12).

Sometimes in my life as a shepherd I got a sheep that was gifted to me as part of my shepherd's wages. (I worked for my father, you see, and I didn't get very much money.) If you go to a sheep or lamb sale, you will very often find that a little lamb will come in and the auctioneer will say, 'Now here's the shepherd's lamb.' It was a gift from the owner of the sheep to the man who was shepherding them. I have seen shepherds, and pretty hard-bitten shepherds too, almost in tears as their lamb was sold.

Because that lamb had been gifted to them it meant a great deal to them, and they spent a lot of time looking after it. No lamb in the place was better looked after than the shepherd's lamb. And so it is with Jesus; we are his gift.

Purchased

But the sheep also belong to him in another way. They are his not only because he has been given them, but because he has purchased them.

Very often shepherds have to go and buy sheep. I had to do that. I can remember spending my twenty-first birthday at a sale in Stirling, buying new sheep. When you brought new sheep on to a place, you had to spend a lot of time on them, because new sheep wandered away. Usually, to improve a flock, you bought expensive sheep, and the very fact that you had paid out a lot for them meant that you looked after them all the better. Sometimes you would get an hour's sleep at night, sometimes not even that. You spent your days and your nights seeing that these beasts did not tumble into a drain or wander off to somebody else or fall over a cliff. Why did you spend so much time on them? Because you had paid a great price for them.

How much more this Shepherd! What was the price that this Shepherd paid for his sheep? The apostle Peter says, 'ye were not redeemed with corruptible things, as silver and gold ... but with the precious blood of Christ' (1 Peter 1:18–19). He bought these sheep by laying down his own life for them.

Are you afraid that you will go to hell? You won't if you are his. The price that he paid will make him watch you very closely. He will not tether you—a shepherd does not do that; it is not good for a sheep. You think that if you were tethered you would be very holy, don't you? No, you wouldn't be, because sin comes from within. He will let you wander sometimes, but he will not let you over the cliff. Eternal life is the gift of God; and because it is God's gift, it is never forfeited. This Shepherd will look after his sheep. He has paid for them.

Born into the flock

Thirdly, he has a right to say '*my* sheep' because, as well as being gifted and bought, they have been *born* into his flock. Now, you see, in an ordinary flock you could not say that a sheep was a gift to me, *and* bought by me, *and* born into my flock, because those things would be contradictory. But the wonder of this flock is that all these things are true of each one of them.

You know, there is a feeling that every shepherd has about a lamb born into his flock, whether he owns his sheep or not. He knows it from the moment of its birth. Although it is twentyone years since I finished shepherding, I can remember lambs that were born in specific places on that hill of two thousand acres where I shepherded. I could look at a sheep sometimes and remember where it had been born two or three years before. Some of them were born in very rough weather, and when you get a lamb born out on the hills of Argyllshire in that kind of weather you have to do something about it. Sometimes I carried them home in my jacket for five miles and warmed them, and then carried them back five miles. So, you see, you did not forget them very easily.

Just before I finished shepherding, I was looking after almost two thousand breeding ewes. Amongst them were a great many I could point to, remembering the day they were born, the place on the hill, the kind of day it was, and what their mother looked like. Sheep *are* different, you know. They are not just a bundle of wool. They all have their individuality, just like people. They even have different eyes and different-coloured faces; some are cheeky-looking and some are nice-looking.

But, you know, although *I* knew where all those sheep were born, I don't think the sheep bothered very much where they were born. Now I often meet Christians and they say to me, 'Oh, Mr MacMillan, I wish I could tell exactly where I had been born again—born into the flock of Christ.' Well, it is nice to know that, but you don't need to know that. If *he* knows that you have been born into his flock, that is what is important.

Let me ask you, Have you been born into the flock of Christ, born again of the Holy Spirit? You notice that the end of Psalm 22 reads, 'They shall come, and shall declare his righteousness unto a people that shall be born'—born into a relationship with him.

So it is a threefold right that Christ the Shepherd has, and that threefold right constitutes the very basis of the relationship. They are '*my* sheep'—that is what matters.

'I know them'

Then he says another thing about them: 'My sheep … *I know them*'. The mark of a good shepherd is that he knows his sheep. If he does not know his sheep he does not last long as a shepherd. He has to know his sheep as individuals, and he has to know the need of individuals. He has to know the ground on which the sheep live and feed.

I have known men who knew their sheep so well that they could recognise them anywhere. One man I remember had sold a hundred lambs in Oban and, travelling in a train three weeks later, he passed a big flat plain called 'the Carse of Stirling', where lambs are fattened and then sold (often at a fat profit). When he got back home, this fellow said to me, 'You know, Douglas, I saw my lambs.' 'Where did you see your lambs?' I asked. 'In among about three thousand other ones in a field at Stirling', he said.

You see, I didn't even think of saying to him, 'How did you know they were your lambs?' There were no earmarks, because for the market they did not mark the lambs they were selling. But

I never thought of asking him that. The man would have looked at me and said, 'Are you daft?' He knew his lambs.

Now it is the same with Christ. This can be a frightening thought, can't it? You would not like the person who is sitting beside you, even if he is your husband or she is your wife, to know all that is going on inside your mind and heart, would you? But somebody does; your Shepherd does. At first thought that can be frightening, especially when we think of our sins and our failures and our disobedience and our lack of love and our coldness. Yet, you know, it is wonderful that the shepherd does know all that is wrong in the life of a sheep, for if he does not know what is wrong he cannot put it right. The better a shepherd knows the illnesses to which a sheep is subject, the better that shepherd will be.

This is true of Christ. He knows your sin—of course he does! He bore our sins in his own body on the tree. He paid the price of the guilt of your sin—and you are afraid to dig it out and show it to him! My friend, he knows it far better than you do. He knows not only its guilt, but he knows the price for this guilt purchased from the righteousness of God, and he paid the price. He knows your sin and mine as we shall never know it, and he paid the price for *all our* sins. He did what we can never do. He knows you far better than you know yourself, and, my friend, you should thank him today that that is so. He knows every failure. He knew every failure away back there at a place called Calvary, and he paid the price willingly.

I remember someone in our area restocking his farm with sheep, and spending almost two years preparing for this. He was preparing against every eventuality and every difficulty he could see in the way of keeping a new herd of sheep. He had all the drains cleaned, all the fences repaired, all the briars cut down and the bracken mown. He did everything that was possible to him to prepare a place where the sheep could live and prosper. How much more the great Shepherd who is Christ the Lord! '*I know them.*'

The Shepherd knows you even when you do not realise it. Do you remember what Psalm 121 says? Let me give you the Scottish metrical version:

I to the hills will lift mine eyes,
From whence doth come mind aid;
My safety cometh from the Lord,
Who heaven and earth hath made.

It goes on to say that his eye is ever upon us; he does not slumber, he does not sleep. He is the one who lives in the mountains, you see.

On our land there was one particular mountain of about 1,500 feet, and from the top of that mountain I could see 'every thistle', as we would say—every area where sheep were kept. I used to go up there with a pair of powerful glasses so that I could survey the whole area. I remember being up there once on an early summer morning, when the lambs were getting big. We were troubled by hill foxes (in 1953, for example, we lost 300 lambs because of foxes), so I was out there at half-past three in the morning with binoculars, a .303 rifle and a shepherd's crook.

I saw something then that I had never seen before and have never forgotten since. Sitting on top of the hill I could see a fox, way down below me in a flat valley, working sheep just the way a dog works. You have sheep-dog trials in Wales, don't you? You know how the dogs 'wear' the sheep, as we say, gathering them up, bunching them together, driving them, and doing all these wonderful things. Well, here was a fox doing the very same thing way down there below me. All the mothers were in a great state of trial, trying to protect their lambs. The fox was actually trying to drive the sheep to a boggy place. He was wanting to get the lambs stuck down, as they were getting big.

I waited, because this fox was working better than any collie I have ever seen. I waited a long time, and the sheep were all distressed and troubled. For them the world was turning upside down, and they had eyes only for the fox. Then, when the time came and I could see the fox really going in for the kill, I did something very, very simple. I put two fingers in my mouth and I whistled. The fox was off like a shot.

Now, you see, the shepherd's eye was on the sheep all the time. He knew precisely what was happening and he had the ability in a moment to shield them from all danger and harm. How much more our Shepherd! He never slumbers; he never sleeps. His eye is on you. He watches you for your good. '*I know them.*' He knows the kind of person you are, he knows your circumstances, and he will suit his grace to meet the very kind of person you are. Are you bad-tempered? Well, he will have a special way of dealing with you. Are you easily tempted? He will have a special way of dealing with you. Are you tempted by one particular sin? He will fit his shepherding of you to his knowledge of you. 'My sheep ... I know them.'

The sheep's viewpoint

We have looked at the sphere of the relationship depicted for us in Psalm 23 from the Shepherd's viewpoint. Let us look now at the other side of the relationship, from the point of view of the sheep. 'My sheep hear my voice ... and they follow me.' Two things are true of every one who is a sheep of Christ. Spurgeon put it very beautifully when he said, 'They have a mark in their ear and a mark in their foot.' That is true.

'*They hear my voice*'
With every sheep that I brought home to take into the flock, the first thing I had to do was to take a big, long, sharp, killing knife.

I was not going to cut their throats, but I was going to mark their ears. In Scotland we call it a 'lug mark'. It was my particular mark, and it marked that sheep out as mine.

Now that is not the kind of mark that Spurgeon meant when he said that the Christian has a mark in his ear. The kind of thing he was talking about was what Jesus has in mind here—'they hear my voice'. There are two words in Greek for hearing, and it is interesting to note that the one that is used here means not simply 'to hear a sound' but 'to hear and to understand'—hearing with understanding. (Gaelic has two words for hearing as well, and makes exactly the same distinction.)

That is a perfect illustration of what happens when God's Spirit begins to work in the life of a sinner. They begin to hear. Psalm 22 was telling us that Christ in his death through the cross was calling. 'My sheep hear my voice.' Every time you hear the gospel, he is calling. Every time you have the thought of righteousness or holiness, he is calling. Every time you have longings to be a better man or woman, the voice of Christ is calling. And suddenly you begin to understand what is happening and to listen.

Understanding

Can I again use a personal illustration? For twenty-one years I listened to the gospel, but I hadn't a clue what the gospel was about. I had listened to the gospel since I was a baby in my mother's arms. It was a Christian home. The preachers on a Sabbath afternoon came to us for their dinner. I was always used to a home that was full of Christian people. I had been told the gospel by my mother and my father, and I had heard the gospel from the pulpit. I used to listen to men saying, 'Now if you want to be a Christian, you must come to Christ', and I used to think, 'What on earth does the man mean?' I used even to say to myself, 'Well, I wish I was preaching there, and I wish I knew what it was to come to Christ. Then I would be able to tell people what to do.' The gospel was just jargon to me, and words like 'Come to Christ—trust in Christ—be born again' did not mean a thing.

Then, all of a sudden, the gospel began to have meaning for me. When a preacher said 'Come to Christ', I knew exactly what he meant. When he said 'Trust your soul to the Lord Jesus', I knew what he meant. When he said 'Christ died for your sins', I thought that was wonderful. What was happening? I was not only hearing with the ear, I was understanding and I was listening, and I was drawing life into my soul. What had happened? I had become a sheep, and I understood the Shepherd's language and knew the Shepherd's voice. The gospel began to have meaning and validity to me.

I shall never forget. I was converted on a Tuesday night and I went to church for the first time for a long time on a Sunday morning. The man was preaching that morning on Psalm 23, and his text was, 'Thou preparest a table before me'. It was a very vivid sermon about how the Lord provided for his people. He was a vivid preacher.

Imagining goblets and dishes, he would lift a huge glass and say, 'What's in this one? Here is the undying love of Christ!' And I would say, 'Great!' It all meant something to me. Why? Because I had been given a new appreciation. 'My sheep hear my voice.' Messages that had been nonsense to me for twenty-one years were making sense; they were valid and real—more real than anything I knew. And it is still the case.

Let me illustrate. Every winter, when November came, we used to take the lambs that had been born in the spring (we call them 'hoggs' in Scotland) down into the park just below the house. It was a big park of about 60 to 80 acres. They were wintered down there in the fields, and they were fed from a long wooden trough where we put food out for them every morning. I left home at the end of August, going to Edinburgh to study—a fellow with heather growing out of his ears! I missed my sheep, and one weekend, when I heard that my brother had had the lambs in for about a month and was feeding them, I said, 'I'm going home to see the sheep.' I had a motor cycle (and was crazy on motor-cycling), so I went home all the way from Edinburgh.

The first morning I was home I said to my brother, 'I'll come down with you and feed the sheep.' When we reached the gate of the park I said to him, 'Now I'll call them.' I started to call them just the way I always did (they were spread all over the park, you see). I called and called, and not a sheep lifted its head! 'Man, that's funny!' I said. I tried again. Then I said, 'You'd better do it yourself!' So he called. His voice was very like mine—so like mine that when a certain young lady whom I got to know better later on used to phone our farm and Malcolm answered, she would think it was I! Many people could not tell the difference between his voice and mine. And yet, as soon as he called, every young lamb in the park lifted its head and ran. Why? My voice was just a sound to them, but my brother's voice meant nice warm food on a cold frosty morning, and so they came. They knew the shepherd's voice.

Identity

It is very difficult to define what a Christian is, but here is one side of the relationship. If you are a Christian, you know that Christ and the gospel have come to have a validity and meaning and purpose for you. I would go further. The gospel has given you an identity.

I said at the beginning that there was no such thing as a shepherd without sheep. But isn't it true that until you live a life that is centred and focused in Christ, you are a sheep without a shepherd, a creature that belongs to nobody? I have never really known a sheep that had no owner. It would be a beast without identity, having nothing against which to know itself. There is no such thing, either, as a Christian who has no Saviour, is there? And until you come to know Christ in the gospel in a personal way, until this relationship is constituted, you are lost, and you do not have identity. But the moment you do know Christ in reality, you then know what it is all about. You know why God has given you life; you know where the world is going; you know that life is worthwhile because God is on the throne.

You see, this is one of the sad things about our day and age. People have no sense of identity or of belonging, and they have no end purpose. They do not know what life is for and what life is about. Can you blame them that they live the way they do? They turn to every kind of thing—'pop' music, drugs, drink, immorality—because they are trying to fill a gap. We criticise them, looking down our noses at them and saying, 'Isn't that terrible?' Yes, but we should expect it. These people have no identity—and, you know, only you and I can bring the gospel to them.

Are we doing it? I have been hearing a lot of talk about longing for revival in Wales. Well, when revival comes to Wales, one of the things that will happen is that Christians will talk to men and women that are lost and without a shepherd. They will cry and mourn and weep over men and women because they are without a shepherd, won't they? Are they doing it yet? Somebody was asking last night, 'When will we know when revival comes to Wales?' When will we know when it comes to Scotland? When we can go down on our knees before God and weep for men that are lost. And they are lost even now in this life, not just over the brink of eternity. They are sheep without a shepherd. Don't sneer at them. Pray for them. Love them in Christ until you bring them to Christ. 'My sheep hear my voice.'

'They follow me'

The other thing that is true of these sheep is that 'they follow me'. Now that is very simple, but it is a very beautiful description of what the Christian life is. I suppose if you asked everyone here what a Christian is, they could give you a different definition and still be within the framework of Scripture. But here is a very simple definition: a Christian is a person who follows Jesus. Do you remember the story of blind Bartimaeus? He was healed, and the last thing that we read of him is this: 'he ... followed Jesus in the way' (Mark 10:52).

This phrase, 'following Jesus', is so descriptive of what a Christian really is that on the west coast of Scotland, the Gaelic-speaking regions, we use it to denominate a Christian. If you were on the Isle of Lewis, for example, and somebody was gloriously converted, you would say, 'So and so has begun to follow', and nobody in Lewis would misunderstand you. 'He is following the gospel' means that God has laid hold of him. God's Spirit is working, a Christian characteristic is appearing, he is following Jesus. Could you get a better definition? Many good things come out of Lewis, and here is one of them!

Often when we are asked to say what a Christian is, we do so in completely unbiblical terms. 'A Christian is someone who goes to chapel or church; or they are Baptists or Presbyterians; or they wear certain clothes or do their hair a certain way; or they don't smoke or drink; or they don't dress like this or listen to that kind of music.' You know, an awful lot of it is sheer rubbish! A Christian is a follower of Jesus, and the fancy clothes and so on can sort themselves out in God's good time. The moment they are born again of the Holy Ghost, they will be clothed in the righteousness of Jesus Christ. That is the most important clothing, isn't it? They *follow*.

Direction

Now do you see what that implies? If they are following, they are being led. Their lives are brought under the sovereign direction of an omnipotent God. God, who knows all things from the

71

beginning to the end, in grace and mercy and love has planned to bring great blessing to every one of his people. They are under his direction, a direction that comes by Christ through the Holy Ghost. Following Jesus means that your life has been brought into purposeful living in accord with his Word.

Have you ever seen a yacht towing a little boat out of a harbour? When they start off, the little boat does not seem to have much connection with the bigger one. There is a long tow-rope and it is just bobbing about. Then the big boat begins to move, and all of a sudden you see the wee one jerking and following. What is happening? It is under the direction of another power, it is being motivated.

That is what happens to a Christian; he is made to follow Jesus. It does not matter who you are; if you are following Jesus you are a Christian. No matter how you feel or what else is true of you, if God in his grace has brought your life under direction and made you follow Christ, then that is one of the best signs you can have. If that is true of you, then you have nothing to be afraid of.

Isn't it wonderful to have a Shepherd like Jesus directing, controlling, managing? I use the word 'management' deliberately. You see, a shepherd is not just a jack of all trades. If he is to be a good shepherd, he has to be a very efficient business manager. He has to know a great deal about diseases, veterinary medicines, how to give injections, and all sorts of other things. What is more, he has to keep very accurate books, because there are people called taxation officers.

You know, you can tell from looking at the sheep how good a manager their shepherd is. When I go north to preach, I usually go by car from Glasgow, and all the way, whether I go by Glencoe or by Perth, I am passing through great sheep country. (Sometimes I sit and watch these black-faced sheep for far too long, and then I'm late!) I can tell pretty accurately by the look of the sheep what kind of man is shepherding and managing them. The sheep reflect the kind of person the shepherd is.

Look at the Manager we have here! Are you reflecting him? There is nobody else in this world who reflects the kind of Shepherd Jesus is, but you who are his sheep. Remember that, as you live for him. You have a wonderful Shepherd, and so you should be a wonderful sheep. Live for him, live your best for him, and let people see what a wonderful Shepherd you have.

Destination

A life that is being led by Jesus and is following Jesus has not only direction but destination. That is what is missing in the lives of most people today. They have no end purpose, no destination. Many of the 'pop' songs of today are propounding this philosophy—I have got nothing to live for; I am travelling and I am going nowhere. It is true of every non-Christian man and woman that they are travelling out into an eternity in which God in his grace and love is not present—outer darkness. But the Christian has a destination. Let people know that; let people know that you are going somewhere, and that you know where you are going.

The Shepherd and his sheep

Who are the sheep of Psalm 23? They are those who follow Jesus. What is the sphere of Psalm 23? It is the relationship constituted between the Shepherd and his sheep. It belongs to the Shepherd first of all. David could only say, 'The LORD is my shepherd', because God in Christ, in his redemptive purpose, was saying of David, 'my sheep'. If you can say today, 'The LORD is my shepherd', you are saying it because God said from eternity, 'my sheep'. You are owned; you have been given identity; your life has direction, and you have a destination. You have a Good Shepherd and he is living—living to be a Shepherd. He moved from death when he came into Psalm 23. He came in as the one whom God had 'brought again from the dead, our Lord Jesus, that great shepherd of the sheep'.

In Psalm 24 he is not only the Great Shepherd, but he is the Chief Shepherd. He is glorified, and the glory of our Lord Jesus is messianic glory, the glory that belongs to his saviourhood, the glory which is his because of the sheep. So, you see, that glory of his is your destination, because he is going to share it with you. That is what makes a shepherd—having sheep.

There is a verse in Psalm 84 which I think sums up all I have been trying to say in relation to Psalms 22, 23 and 24. It says this: 'For the LORD God is a sun and shield: the LORD will give grace and glory: no good thing will he withhold from them that walk uprightly' (verse 11). 'The LORD will give grace'—he has done that; that is what Psalm 22 is all about. And then 'the LORD will give glory'—Psalm 24, you see.

Let me say this. He never ever gives glory until he gives grace first. Equally, he never gives grace but he infallibly gives glory. He gives grace and he gives glory. Here we have the beginning— the gateway of the cross into the experience and life of the sheep; and we also have the destination—glory. And what is in between? Psalm 23. He gives grace and he gives glory, and in between these two it is true that 'he will withhold no good thing from them that walk uprightly'. That is what Psalm 23 is about. It is about the giving by the Shepherd of every blessing that the sheep will ever need.

3

Feeding the flock

'The LORD is my shepherd; I shall not want. He maketh me
to lie down in green pastures: he leadeth me beside the still
waters. He restoreth my soul: he leadeth me in the paths of
righteousness for his name's sake'—(Psalm 23:1–3)

U p to this point we have been looking at Psalm 23 in a broader
context, putting it into its setting in relation to the rest of
Scripture and in relation to real, living Christian experience. Christ—
Jehovah-Jesus—is our Shepherd, and every one who has been
brought by the Spirit of God into a living, personal relationship
with him is his sheep. Christianity is not merely knowing a set of
doctrines. The heart or core of a Christian's faith is that he is brought
into union, into a living relationship, with Christ Jesus, his Lord and
Shepherd; and that means, of course, into a living relationship with
the Triune God, Father, Son and Holy Spirit.

Theologians speak of the *ordo salutis* (the order in which God
deals with us in grace), and sometimes they differ as to what is
the very first work that God does with a sinner when he brings
him to Christ. I myself believe that the very first thing that
happens is union with Christ. Some theologians would put faith
before that; others would put regeneration before it. But I am
talking not of a fixed time-sequence, but of an order—a logical
order—in God's work.

It seems to me that a soul which is dead cannot exercise faith.
Before the soul can trust in Christ, there has to be a quickening of

the Holy Spirit, a work of God. So I would say that regeneration precedes faith, and the first act of the living soul is to rest on Christ.

But I would say also that there is something else before regeneration, and that is union with Christ. We are united to him in the purpose of God from eternity, and when the Holy Spirit comes, he comes to begin a work of renewal and regeneration. So, although I would not be dogmatic about this, I believe that the very first thing the Spirit does is to link us into union with Christ. You see, it would be impossible for the soul to live in isolation from the life of Christ, for Christ is our life. The moment the soul springs to life, there is union to Christ; or, we could say, in union to Christ the Spirit brings the soul to life.

Now I say that because this wonderful psalm, inspired by the Holy Ghost through the 'Poet Laureate' of the Scriptures, speaks about a relationship. It speaks of what a person is only in a living relationship to God's Shepherd, the Lord Jesus Christ.

Linked to the Shepherd

The first thing we notice in the psalm is the sense of serenity and confidence which pervades it. Here is a soul that is resting in God, and a soul that *knows* it is resting in God; a soul that not only knows the Shepherd, but *knows* that it knows the Shepherd. Because it knows the Shepherd, because it can say 'The LORD— Jehovah-Jesus—is *my* Shepherd', then it can go on to say all the other things. I think it was Martin Luther who said that the essence of the blessing of being a Christian lay in the ability to use personal pronouns. The use of the words 'I' and 'my' and 'me' is only possible because we are linked into the life of Christ.

But there are sides to a relationship, and really the psalm is not first of all about the sheep; it is about the Shepherd. Every single word in the psalm depends upon the character, the authenticity and the reality of the shepherdhood of the one of whom it is speaking in its opening breath—the Lord! But whilst the psalm is first of all about the Shepherd, you cannot imagine a shepherd who has no sheep, and you cannot imagine a Saviour who is not bringing in the lost. He came 'to seek and to save'.

That is the essence of the message of Ezekiel 34: 'I will both search my sheep, and seek them out ... I will seek that which was lost' (verses 11,16). Here is the very essence of what revival is: it is a revival not of our work but of his—'Revive *Thy* work, O Lord.' You see, his work is a coming and a bringing in of the sheep that were scattered. It is the moulding of them and the guiding of them into a flock, into a people who will be the people of God. The summit of it all is found in the last verses of Ezekiel 34: 'I the LORD their God am with them, and ... they ... are my people ... And ye my flock ... are men, and I am your God.'

That, too, it seems to me, is the constant emphasis of the closing chapters of the Book of Revelation. The substance of it is simply this: 'he will dwell with them, and they shall be his people, and God himself shall be with them, and be their God' (Revelation 21:3). But you already have that ultimate perfection, in reality and in essence, if not in totality of degree, the moment the life is linked to the Shepherd. If 'The LORD is *my* shepherd', that guarantees the fact that one day I will be in the place Revelation speaks of, where 'I will be his God, and he shall be my son' (21:7).

The Shepherd through the eyes of the sheep

Now the wonder of this psalm is that, although its priority and emphasis are on the Shepherd, it speaks about the sheep. What it does for us really is this: it allows us to look at the Shepherd through the eyes of the sheep. That is essential, for only those who have been redeemed by his grace, only those who have tasted of his love, know what Christ is like. Listen to the unconverted man talking about Jesus. He may know much about him, and yet in all his talk you don't see the loveliness of Christ, do you? But here God allows us to see Christ through the eyes of those who have been redeemed by him. Through the eyes of the sheep he lets us see the tenderness and kindness, and sometimes the stern discipline, of the Shepherd.

Really, we are dealing with something very wonderful here: we are dealing not only with a living Shepherd, but with a living sheep. Psalm 23 is about those who have been quickened unto grace; it belongs to God's people. So often this psalm is abused because other people take it and try to take comfort from it; but it does not belong to them. The reason why we have spent some time before coming near the psalm is that I wanted you to be very sure who the Shepherd was, and who the sheep are to whom this psalm and the blessings it enumerates belong.

Recognition

'The LORD is my shepherd.' The very first thing here is *recognition.* 'The Lord is my shepherd,' and I know him as my Shepherd. What an emphasis there is in the New Testament on knowing God and knowing Jesus Christ! What is life eternal? When the New Testament talks of eternal life, it is not talking of quantity of life, nor of mere endurance. Those who are to be lost and without eternal life will have immortality; their life will go on. But eternal life is a quality of life, a life that is rooted in God. It is spoken of in this way: 'This is life eternal, that they might know thee, the only true God, and Jesus Christ, whom thou hast sent' (John 17:3).

There is something lovely about old saints; you see the grace of God wonderfully in them. Paul was an old man, an old saint of God, when he prayed this prayer: 'That I may know him, and the power of his resurrection, and the fellowship of his sufferings' (Philippians 3:10). You may pray to God 'that I may know him', but will you pray too that you may know the fellowship of his sufferings and conformity with his death? That was Paul's longing—to know him. You see, a personal relationship is not a static thing; it is a living, dynamic thing, and therefore it is subject to increase.

I would guess my wife knows me quite well. She has known me for nearly nineteen years now as a wife, and she knows me a lot better now than the first couple of weeks we were married. Why? Because her knowledge of me has kept pace with the length of our relationship.

Let me ask you a very simple but a very searching question. How many years have you been a Christian? Has your knowledge, your personal knowledge of the one with whom you are in relationship, kept pace with the duration of your relationship? Do you know Jesus better today than you knew him the day you found him as your Saviour? To know him! 'The Lord is my shepherd', and because he is *my* Shepherd, I am getting to know him better all the time; and in knowing him I am in possession of eternal life, I am a living sheep.

I have already spoken of how wonderful Christian assurance is—not only knowing him, but knowing that we know him. Now I want to take the other side of the relationship. Do you often let the Lord Jesus know that you know him? You may think that a very strange thing for the preacher to say. Let me illustrate. You remember a day at Caesarea Philippi when Jesus began to question his disciples, 'Whom do men say that I am?' 'Well,' they said, 'some people say that you are Elijah, and some say that you are a prophet, and some say this and some say that.' Then Jesus came spearing in and said, 'But who do *you* say that I am?' Peter spoke out, and I think he spoke for them all: 'Thou art the Christ, the Son of the living God.'

I believe that the human heart of our Saviour rejoiced at this. (We are so concerned for his divinity, as it has been attacked so much, that all too often we forget that he is the *man* Christ Jesus.)

He said, 'Blessed art thou, Simon Bar-jona: for flesh and blood hath not revealed it unto thee, but my Father' (Matthew 16:17). Why did Jesus rejoice? Because he knew that he was known. He saw (if I can put it like this) that God the Holy Spirit had opened the eyes of Peter and the other disciples, and that now they were piercing through the disguise of his humanity and were seeing the God-Man.

I remember one day, almost three years after I had left my shepherding to go to Edinburgh to study, that I was back home for summer holidays, and working with my brother. We were looking at lambs in one sheep pen that had been separated from their mothers in another pen, and I was standing with my hands just dangling idly by my side, admiring some of the lambs and despairing of others.

Suddenly I felt a sheep's nose nuzzling into my hand. I looked down, and there was a sheep almost five years old—a sheep that for six months I had looked after as a lamb, taking it home to the farm and feeding it with a bottle every so often. Although it went back to the hill after six months, that sheep would always come to me. The other sheep knew their shepherd, but they would not come as close as that to him. But this one would. That sheep had not seen me for almost three years. She was in from the hill, and she lived on a part of the hill that was almost three miles away from the farm. I was standing with my brother, and he had been the shepherd for three years. Yet I looked around and here she was! I was thrilled. Why? Because she knew me; and she was letting me know that she knew me.

How often, just going down on our knees or while walking along the street, do you and I say, 'Lord Jesus, I am glad I know you'? Love of any kind loves to know that it is loved in return. Can we ask less, or expect less, of the kind of love with which God has loved us in Christ? How often do you let your soul relax, and say, 'O Lord Jesus, I love you'? We so often say, 'Thank you,

Jesus, for loving me', but how often do we just love him back in return?

Those of you who are married will understand that wives have a strange psychology. You do everything in your power to show them that you love them, but you don't actually speak it out. You do all you can—you even wash the dishes sometimes!—and then she will say, 'But do you really love me?' And you reply, 'Of course. Can't you see what I'm doing for you? Do you think I'd still be here if I didn't?' And she will say, 'But I like to hear you saying it.' Well, how much more the love of Christ!

The rest of the flock

Let me ask you something else. Do you love Christ's people? This is one of the marks of being a Christian, according to John, the 'apostle of love'. 'We know', he says, 'that we have passed from death unto life, because we love the brethren' (1 John 3:14). Do you ever tell your fellow Christians that you love them in Christ? Or do you ever tell them by your looks? Sometimes you can tell by the way someone shakes your hand that he loves you in the Lord Jesus Christ. And that tells you that you really are a sheep, that you are one of the flock, that you both have the same Shepherd, and that the love of Christ is shed abroad in your hearts. A lot of nice things have been said to me since I came into this conference; but the nicest thing—and it is something I will remember and take with me to the end of the journey—has been this. Someone came up to me and said the best thing he could have said. He said, 'Man, I love you.' I had never seen the man, never spoken with him, until I came to this conference. But, you know, I can say back in return, 'Man, I love you too.'

It is the nature of sheep to fellowship with sheep. At one period in my shepherding a white goat appeared on our hill. Where it came from I do not know to this day, but it must have been brought up with some pet lambs somewhere and wandered on to our hill. It was a very strange goat—it thought it was a sheep! But the funny thing was that not one sheep on my hill believed that that goat was a sheep, and they would have nothing to do with it. Why? Because sheep fellowship with sheep. A sheep has to be reared out of her environment before she will have fellowship with any other kind of animal—a sheep does not like goats.

Christian fellowship means being part of the flock. That is one of the things that is a marvel of God's tenderness towards us. I always think there is something wrong with the Christian who does not seek fellowship with other Christians. I had the privilege, under God, of pasturing many young people for almost eight years, and whenever I saw difficulties in the lives of these young Christians, one of the first signs was that they stopped coming to the fellowship meetings, and they stopped seeking fellowship in Christ. I used to think back to my shepherding experiences. What did a shepherd look for automatically every time he was on his hill, but for a sheep that had separated herself from the rest of the flock? He knew that there was something wrong with her. How much time do you spend in the fellowship of believers?

My father, in a sense, was the jack of all trades in our area. When I was a little boy he was a building contractor, but he was also the local blacksmith, shoeing all the horses and doing all kinds of things. We went into a farm when I was almost eleven, but he carried on as the local blacksmith. Just after I was converted, when he was quite an old man, we were doing something in the smithy on the farm, and the fire on the blacksmith's hearth was alight with little lumps of coal. I was turning the handle, blowing the bellows, doing the hard graft, and he said, 'Douglas, I want you to look at something.' With a pair of tongs he took just one coal off the fire, put it on the anvil and said, 'Watch that!' It came out glowing red, almost white, and we stood and watched it on the anvil. Do you know what happened? It began to turn blue, greeny-blue, and then black. He said, 'If we leave it long enough, it will be cold. Always seek Christian fellowship.' I learned a very important lesson there that day. Christian fellowship is a means of grace; we are part of a flock of living sheep.

So this psalm begins with recognition: first of all, recognition by the Shepherd, then, recognition of the Shepherd; thirdly, recognition of one another in the Shepherd as part of the Shepherd's flock.

Satisfaction

This leads on to *satisfaction*. 'The Lord is my shepherd; I shall not want'—or 'I shall lack nothing.' Yet this word means more than mere lack: it means just what the word 'want' originally meant. It means that I will not be discontented with my lot. I will not be hungering and craving after things that God has forbidden me, because I will find my all, my fullness, in the one who is my Shepherd. My knowledge that I shall suffer no lack will give me contentment. Do you remember how Paul put it? He said, 'Godliness with contentment is great gain'—and so it is, because it leads to a quiet soul, confident that 'I shall not want for anything.'

One of the things that is fundamental to the whole business and profession of a shepherd is this: enough passion to see that his sheep will have all that they need, and enough sense to see that they will not get what will harm or destroy them. That is the kind of shepherd, and that is the kind of satisfaction, that the Christian believer finds in Christ. 'I shall not want.'

Do you see the logic of cause and consequence here? There is wonderful logic in Scripture—great, powerful, strong, intellectual reasoning. Take God's Word and draw the consequences from it. Here it is: if the Lord is my Shepherd, *can* I want? *will* I want? will I lack anything that I need to bring me safe home?

The Bible is full of that kind of wonderful logic. For example, 'because I live, ye shall live also' (John 14:19); 'Fear not: for I have redeemed thee' (Isaiah 43:1); 'If God be for us, who can be against us?' (Romans 8:31). It is great philosophy, great logic, the logic and philosophy of grace. Learn to use your Scripture, allow God to fortress and garrison your heart with the great strength of his promises and of his logical grace. The inevitable consequence of the Lord being my Shepherd is that 'I shall not want', and, you see, the rest of the psalm really is a development of that consequence. Every blessing that is enumerated is a reassurance, an assertion that you will not 'want'.

Let us look at some of the things that he begins to enumerate to demonstrate the truth of what he has just asserted. And remember that we are talking about sheep. This psalm convinces me that it was written by David (though some people think otherwise), because the man who wrote this psalm knew sheep inside out. I think it was John MacNeil, the famous Scottish evangelist, who was once asked, 'Who do you think, John, wrote the twentythird Psalm?' 'Man,' he said, 'I think I wrote it myself.' The man said to him, 'What do you mean, you wrote it yourself?' He said, 'Well, every time I read it I feel as if I have to say to myself, "Well, David said it before me, but I was really going to say it myself."' That shows how the psalm fits us, or, to put it another way, it shows how the Christian fits the psalm. The Christian can go to any part of Scripture and find that God's Word is shaped for him, as it is shaped for nobody else.

'He maketh me to lie down'

What a picture of satisfaction is here—'He maketh me to lie down'! If I were not a shepherd, I think I would wonder what on earth the psalmist meant by these words. But because I am a shepherd, I know that one of the most difficult things to attain among a flock of sheep is to get them to lie down. There are four things that will keep a sheep from lying down, and I think we can take these four things and apply them in Christian experience.

Fear

The first thing is *fear*. A sheep that is afraid will never lie down. Sheep came right around our farmhouse, and if a strange car drew up, the sheep that were lying there would all stand up and look, as if to say, 'Who's arriving now?' They did that before *we did!* If a strange dog came out of that car, their eyes would get big and their ears would go forward and they were ready to be off. A sheep that is afraid will not lie down, and a sheep is very easily frightened.

So is a Christian, because sin brought fear along in its wake. 'I heard thy voice ... and I was afraid ... and I hid myself' (Genesis 3:10). Why did Adam say that? Because he had sinned. Sin had come home to his mind and his heart, and fear is one of the strange but inevitable results of sin. We see that at every level of human life, and it tends to follow the Christian believer.

One of the things that Christ wants to do in your life is to dispel fear and give you rest and quiet. 'Come unto me ... and I will give you rest' (Matthew 11:28). Only Christ can take away our fears. A knowledge of theology cannot do it; even a bare knowledge of the Word cannot do it. The lovely presence of our lovely Saviour, that does it every time.

Antagonism

Then there is something else that keeps a sheep from lying down, and that is *antagonism* from within the flock. We have what I used to call 'bully-boy' sheep. If it was a hen-house they would call it the 'pecking order'! There is always a sheep that wants to be the big sheep, that wants to be the boss, that wants to shine, that wants to say to the shepherd, 'Look at me, I'm looking after all the others.'

You find the same thing in almost every congregation of Christian believers. I knew one woman (I believe she is in glory now), and her job took her through various congregations in our denomination in Scotland. In every one of them she wanted to be the big sheep, and in every one of them she caused a lot of heartache and anguish. Don't want to be a big sheep! They are a perfect pest to the shepherd. Sometimes I had to get hold of a sheep and chastise her and say, 'You leave that alone!'—and the sheep would know.

When sheep lie down, as the psalmist tells us, they want to lie down in green grass; they would not lie down in the heather. So you would find all the sheep gathered together on green knolls and lying there. But sometimes I would see them standing up, and I would know right away what was wrong with them. I would say, 'Ay, ay, one of the bully-boys at it again.' There she would be, the big sheep, showing what a fine sheep she was. She would go up to a sheep that was lying down, and she would stamp her foot and dilate her eyes and look very fierce, and you would see the other poor sheep getting up and running off four or five yards. Then she would go to another sheep, and so on until she had the whole flock up, and she would not stop until she saw me. I had a special whistle for that kind of sheep! Once I had whistled she would calm down, and in a wee while they would all be lying down again. Sheep will not lie down if there is any kind of antagonism or frustration or tension.

Now just think how often we allow tensions to arise in ourselves and antagonisms to simmer within us against our brothers and our sisters in Christ! Yet we are warned against this—'lest any root of bitterness springing up trouble you' (Hebrews 12:15). As soon as these things surface in our hearts we should be taking them to the Shepherd and putting them under the blood of Christ, because they are the root of sin. Yet how often, even among godly people, jealousies arise! You have the 'butting order' we shepherds spoke of. You get it even among ministers—professional jealousy: 'I wish I could preach the way *he* does! But God has not made you that kind of preacher, and maybe you should be thankful for this. Let's be content not to be big guns, but to be what God has meant us to be, and thank him for the least gift that he has given us.

Annoyance

There is something else that will keep a sheep from lying down, and it is something to which a shepherd has to pay very careful attention. A sheep that is *annoyed by flies or insects* will not lie down.

I remember in the summer months when I began shepherding (I was still under 14 years of age), I had to spend the long, hot summer days walking the hills watching for sheep that were coming under the 'strike', as we called it. Every ten days we had to take every single sheep on our hill and spray it and dip it and powder its head, etc. We used stuff called 'MacDougalls' Dip', and I used to think that instead of it frightening away the flies, the flies bred on it! If they got maggot strike, sheep could die; it was horrible—they could be eaten away! Just for the flies to be around the sheep was enough. This would lift them off their feet, set them running, and make them hide in bushes where they would often get caught.

Again, in the Christian life we allow things that are really just insects, trifles, details, to annoy and frustrate us. What should we do with them? Take them to the Shepherd, because they are disturbers of our peace. It may be worry about tomorrow or the day after tomorrow; it may be worry about how on earth you are going to manage to preach for another winter to the same people, or how you are going to manage to listen for another winter to the same dry minister. We worry about the future, about what may or may not happen. These are the flies of Satan, to distract us and annoy us and disturb our rest.

Hunger

Then there is a fourth thing: a sheep that is *hungry will* never lie down. 'He maketh me to lie down'—he has led them into the finest pastures. You have often seen a sheep lying down in green grass, but one kind of sheep that you have never seen doing that is a hungry sheep. A hungry sheep will not lie down; it will stand there and eat. Then, when it has eaten to satisfaction, it will lie down, and you have never seen such a picture of contentment!

What is the green grass for the Christian? What does the Shepherd feed his sheep on? The Word of God and the means of grace. Green grass is always living grass, full of sap and nourishment and good for sheep to feed on. The living Word of God is where the soul must feed.

Young Christians, let me say something to you. Do you want to get to know the Shepherd better? He is here, in this Book. If you want to feed on him, do it from his Word. Why do young Christians find the Christian way difficult? Why do they get cold and wander back into the world? Why do they become afraid and not make a strong and uncompromising stand for Christ? Nearly always because they are neglecting God's Word.

Peter tells us to 'grow in grace, and in the knowledge of our Lord and Saviour Jesus Christ' (2 Peter 3:18). How do you grow in grace and knowledge? It is by the Word that you grow. Don't feed a sheep, and it will not grow. Don't feed a Christian, and he will not grow either. The Shepherd's concern is that you should be often in your green pastures.

One of the things that strikes me when I read the Puritans is how these men knew the Word of God. They could quote and quote and quote, and they did not have a man called Cruden behind them! They found out where things were and they found it out for themselves. Read the Puritans, and do so with your Bible in your right hand and the Puritan in your left. Read Louis Berkhof too—he is worth reading—but read him with your

Bible in your hand. When you see Scripture references, look them up. Make God's Word your own, don't take it always at second hand.

That is what is wrong with half our preaching. We go to William Hendriksen, and instead of taking the Bible along with us we leave it on the desk. William Hendriksen is one of the best commentators of the present day; read him all you can, but read him *through* the Scriptures. Use the helps that God has given you, but remember they are *helps*. Make the Bible the primary thing, because here are the green pastures of God's living Word.

Still waters

The psalmist then goes on to say, 'He leadeth me beside the still waters.' I think that is a beautiful picture. Remember that the country he was living in was not like our own; it was very short of water. They only got rain twice in the year, the early rain and the latter rains. What a precious thing water was, especially to our shepherd! People say to me, 'Surely sheep don't drink water.' Well, a sheep has to drink water or it will not survive. A sheep is made up of 70 per cent fluid—and there is a lot of fluid in you too. We have to have it because it keeps tissue healthy and builds muscle.

At certain seasons of the year a sheep does not have to drink much water because it gets the water in the dew—'still water' coming down. I remember going out in the early spring and early summer at three and four o'clock in the mornings. I was shepherding in the most westerly point on the British mainland, where we had a later sunrise than they had on the south or east coast. As soon as the sun rose you would see the sheep coming down off the top of the hills into the valleys where the green grass was. You would sometimes see whole plains or moors glittering with dew, looking like a field of pearls, and there the sheep would eat and drink at the same time. God promises, 'I will be as the dew unto Israel' (Hosea 14:5); such is his gentleness in feeding the sheep and nourishing them and leading them on.

Then there is something else which tells me that this psalmist knew his sheep. A sheep will never drink out of a fast-flowing stream. I discovered that in a very simple way. When we were bringing our sheep into the farm, we used to have to gather them and drive them down the hill. Coming from the furthest corner of our hill, we used to have to ford two streams or 'wee burns' with them; and after being driven on a warm day for almost three miles in a huge bunch, the sheep would sometimes be so thirsty that their tongues would literally be hanging out. However, at the first stream we forded there was a lot of gravel and stones. It was a fast-flowing stream, with many ripples, and not a single sheep—not even a thirsty one—would stop to drink in it. I often wondered about this. But the next stream we came to, just half a mile further on, was a very broad ford where the water hardly moved, and at these 'still' waters *every* sheep would stop and drink. I don't know why—perhaps it was just that the water ran up its nose—but the sheep did not like fast-flowing water.

The Word and the Spirit

This man knew his sheep, and he knew his Shepherd, too. He knew God, and he knew he had to have not merely the bare Word, but God coming in the Word and with the Word. He had not only to eat, he had to drink at the same time.

Water is very often used in Scripture as a symbol for the Holy Spirit. God promised Israel that he would send forth his Holy Spirit 'as floods over thirsty ground'. What a beautiful picture! Of course, our need of water is always there; we need the Holy Spirit to teach us; we need him every time we go to the Word. A Bible read without prayer for the life and the teaching of the Holy Spirit is worse (and I say this after a lot of thought) than a Bible not read at all.

Why do I say that? Let me try and illustrate. On part of our shore, the western part of it, there were very steep cliffs which ran almost sheer down into the sea. If you stood and leaned over them with your stick, they curved away underneath you in places. I suppose they would be three or four hundred feet high, but they were broken up and there were ledges and wee tracks on them that only a sheep could use. On those ledges there grew a very green kind of grass. A sheep, just like ourselves, fancies the grass on the other side, and the grass in the most difficult and dangerous places always looks the best. The preacher in the next church down the road is always a lot better than your own, too. The grass is always greener on the other side. How foolish we are!

Our sheep used sometimes to go down these tracks on to the cliffs; they could get down, but very often they could not get back. I remember once some lobster-fishermen ringing us and saying, 'Douglas, we were way round the point today and we saw one of your sheep in the cliff on a ledge.' So my brother and I had to set out over the hills to the cliffs, and we found her away down the cliff on a big ledge with very green grass on it. The green grass had been nibbled down, for she had been on it a long time, perhaps four to seven days or even longer. You see, she could jump down on to the ledge, but she could not jump the seven feet back. And you know, Christian believers, it is always easier to get into a sticky wicket than it is to get out of it. Remember that!

Well, she had had plenty to eat, but nothing to drink, and although we had managed to rescue her, she died two days later. Why? Well, I opened her up and found that all the grass she had eaten had hardened into a solid ball. Ultimately, instead of nourishing her, it had choked life out because there was no fluid. She was what we would describe in medical terms as completely dehydrated, and she could not use the food she had eaten.

The Word and prayer

I believe that one of the curses in the church today is a Bible that is read and not prayed over, and I believe that one of the weaknesses in our preaching today—and we have to recognise them—is preaching that is not prayed over, and sermons that are prepared without prayer. I feel that that is my greatest weakness in my own ministry. But this should not be.

I can never forget the man who was my minister when I left home to begin study, and who is now in glory. He was Kenneth N. Taylor, an Englishman and a great man, a great preacher. He said to me before I left home, when I began preaching: 'Douglas, I want to say something to you. If I was asked to preach a sermon within an hour, I would want to spend three-quarters of the time on my knees before God, and only a quarter of an hour with the commentators.' He was saying, 'Divide your time wisely.' He told me that he had sometimes put as many as 30 hours of work into one sermon. How much of that time was prayer I don't know, but it showed in his preaching. There was an unction and a dew coming down when Kenneth Taylor was preaching, and there are people here today who could testify to that same truth.

This is not just for preachers; it is the same for those who are hearing and reading the Scriptures. Take time! I said the dew was there in the early morning. Do you know that very often before 7.30 on a summer's morning, and certainly by 8.30, the dew was gone? The sheep had to be out early to catch it. When you read through the biographies of the great saints of God—Spurgeon, McCheyne, the great Scottish Covenantors—invariably you find one thing: they got up to spend time with God before they ever went near men.

Young Christians, let me say this to you. I believe that if you are faithful in having a time of prayer and Bible reading, even if you only read and meditate on two verses before you begin your day, then God will keep you and feed you, and he will make you grow and go on. I have ministered among young people for a long time, and I have never yet met one person who backslid and grew cold but they confessed to me (at least they did by the time they were returning) that their backsliding began when they stopped praying and when they stopped reading the Bible with prayer. That is where all backsliding begins.

Why should we seem to think today that periods of coldness and backsliding are inevitable? They are not. The Shepherd does not want them. He can feed us and make us grow, and he wants to do it. 'He maketh me to lie down in green pastures: he leadeth me beside the still waters.' *He* does it, you see—recognise that! Without him we can do nothing.

The means of grace

I have to recognise that every time I go to a pulpit. (God help me the day that I don't recognise it.) I have to recognise it every time I go to my Bible, every time I attempt to witness. But I have to recognise something else too: 'I can do all things through Christ who strengthens me.' How does he strengthen me? In all the means of grace—conferences like this, worship on the Lord's Day, the prayer meeting in the middle of the week.

I cannot understand Christians who do not go to prayer meetings. After I was converted I would finish a day's work very often at seven o'clock in the evening, and then I would motorcycle seven miles to a prayer meeting, and I did not think I was doing anything splendid. I quite honestly cannot understand professing Christians who do not want the fellowship of their fellow believers, and of their shepherd, and of the shepherd's Shepherd, in the prayer meeting and the Bible study.

Restoration

Here, then, there is recognition and satisfaction, and also restoration. Is restoration necessary? Ah yes! 'All we like sheep have gone astray.' There is no animal I know that can stray as easily or as readily as a sheep, and I have come to think that Christians are very like sheep. I have come to think this first of all because of my own heart's experience, and then from what I know of other Christians' experiences. 'I wandered far away from God', says one hymn-writer. We know it is true, every one of us, and the sad thing is that some of us are slow and loath to believe that he is ready to restore us.

My friend, if you have wandered far away from God, do you know what is happening? Your Shepherd is more concerned over you than he is over any other member of his flock. Jesus illustrated that: he leaves the ninety and nine, and he will go out after the one that is lost.

Half my time as a shepherd was spent in concern over sheep that strayed. I knew there were some sheep far more liable to stray than others. You got to know them, and eventually you began to know the kind of places where you would have to look for them. There are some Christians the same. If you were going to have fellowship with them, you would have to go to a cocktail bar (and I'm not saying something that I don't know anything about). There are Christians who are mixing with the world, and you would have to go to a dance hall or a theatre to find them. Well, I ask you! But the Shepherd does it, and he restores their souls.

A 'cast' sheep

You know, when I read this word my mind goes to what we call 'cast' or 'coped' sheep. A sheep can very easily lie down and get into a position where it simply cannot regain its feet without the help of the shepherd. Such a sheep was called 'cast', and there were two things that would make a sheep a cast sheep. One was this: it chose the nicest, softest hollow to lie in. The sheep that wanted an easy bed was always in danger, because she would lie down and sometimes stretch her legs, and then the balance of equilibrium would be lost and she could not get her feet back on to the ground. She would scrape the ground and sometimes tear up all the grass, but she could not get back on to her feet. The longer she lay there, the greater her danger. Gases would build up, causing tension, making the sheep blow out and cutting off the blood supply, especially to the place where she needed it most—her legs. You know what it is like to have a bad stomach; well, the sheep had three of them to contend with, and that was something! The longer she stayed there, the more difficult it became for her to regain her feet.

You see this in Christians too—the Christian who is out for the easy option, who wants the soft number in life. The shepherd who becomes wise to the fact that the sheep looks for a soft hollow chases her out of it, and Christ will do the same. He will not allow you to have a soft option; he knows the danger this is to you.

There was something else that made a sheep become a cast sheep, and that was when a sheep's fleece got too heavy for it. It would lie down, poor sheep, and its fleece would have become so heavy, with bits of bushes and wood and all kinds of foreign matter caught up in it, that it would get cast. This would happen especially the month before the shearing was due.

A fleece that is growing big like that is old wool, and in Scripture old wool, or wool of any kind, very often signifies uncleanness. The high priest, when he went into the Holy of Holies, was not allowed to have one thread of wool about him; he had to have linen.

You know, Christians grow old fleeces. 'Oh yes,' you say, 'yes, of course I know the Lord's blessing. I remember two years ago as though it were this evening.' Well, it's time you were sheared, my friend, because you've got two fleeces on you. Sheep grow one every year. If you have become too mixed up with the world, and you refuse to retain the separation that Christ has made, then, friend, you are in danger.

What did the shepherd do with the sheep that 'coped' because she had become too woolly? For a month before the shearing was due, I always carried a pair of sheep shears, stuck into a pocket. When I had a sheep that was day after day getting turned over on its back and unable to get up, I would say there was nothing else for it but to shear it. It was a difficult job because of what we call the 'rise' (the new growing wool that lifted the old fleece and allowed the sheep to be sheared). This would be so tight that you could hardly get the shears into it. But you *would shear* it, because you knew that if you did not it would die. The sheep was uncomfortable because she had been shorn too closely. There was a danger that she would get sunburnt, but sunburn was better than death!

Our Shepherd has to do the same kind of thing. He will not allow you to destroy your soul, nor his work, and he will take you and shear you. He will take away, perhaps, a sense of his own presence and comfort and blessing, and leave you with nothing until he brings you back to himself. There is a very solemn word in Jeremiah:

Hast thou not procured this unto thyself, in that thou hast forsaken the LORD thy God, when he led thee by the way? ... Thine own wickedness shall correct thee, and thy backslidings shall reprove thee: know therefore and see that it is an evil thing and bitter

—I wish I could impress this on every young believer! It is not only an evil but a *bitter* thing—

that thou hast forsaken the LORD thy God, and that my fear is not in thee, saith the Lord GOD of hosts (2:17,19). 'He restoreth my soul.' And the restoration is often worse than the first coming to Christ.

'He leadeth me'

'He leadeth me in the paths of righteousness.' He leads in straight paths—'without [holiness] no man shall see the Lord' (Hebrews 12:14). God's ways are ways of uprightness. When we walk with God, we are walking with the Holy One of Israel and we have to walk in obedience to his commandments.

A sheep does not make straight tracks for itself. If you see sheep walking in a straight line, you can be sure of one thing: the shepherd is driving them or leading them. The wonderful thing about walking in obedience to God is this, that we are being led. I have already talked about following. Let me talk now about leading. If we are following Jesus, then we are being led, and it is a lot easier to follow than it is to lead. Perhaps the trouble with many of us is that we try and go out in front and clear the way for ourselves. But we have to stay in behind Jesus and follow him, in obedience to all his demands upon us in his work.

Let me use a final illustration. I remember one winter, about November, we had been late in bringing the young sheep down into the parks, and they were still on the mountains. An early snowstorm came, and a gale of wind with it, and we had to go off into the mountains to get the sheep.

We were walking against a blizzard—a very difficult thing to do. You cannot see where you are going, as there is snow in your eyes; you can hardly breathe, as there is snow in your throat; it is pouring on to your person, and your coat becomes caked with it. Now I was walking up a mountain track which I knew inside out, but I was having to watch every inch and fight for every step of progress I made. I was doing it for one reason only: I was concerned about all those young sheep.

Coming behind me was my brother, the one that is on the farm still. He was, and still is, a big, hefty fellow, and very strong. (I was one of four boys and two girls. I was called the 'wee fellow', and the one walking behind me that day was called the 'big fellow'.) Suddenly, when I was just about on the point of saying, 'I think we'll pack it in', I felt a tap on my shoulder, and my brother (who must have realised what was happening) said to me, 'I'll go in front for a while.'

So he came round me and I walked in behind him. And, you know, it was as if I had suddenly arrived in a different world! I would hardly have known that it was snowing at all, and I certainly would not have known there was a breath of wind. There was this big fellow in front of me, and all I had to do to keep going was very simple—I just watched his feet and put my feet where his feet had been. I knew that if there was a bog there, he could be up to his neck in it before I would be!

I also discovered something else: the closer I kept behind him, the easier it was for me. The moment I fell back, even if it was only two steps, I was beginning to battle on my own, and I would have to hurry and catch up.

If we only follow Jesus afar off, the same thing happens; we are struggling on our own. Follow closely, walk with him, and you will find that he takes the brunt of everything. 'He leadeth me.' The 'paths of righteousness' sometimes make us afraid, but when we know that our Shepherd is leading us in love, then the paths of righteousness are lit up with the glory of his love.

'for his name's sake'
And why does he do it?—'for his name's sake'. He has hung the glory, yes, and he has hung the honour of his name as Saviour, on your salvation and on his shepherding of you. Your soul is vitally important to him because he loves you. But it is important for another reason also. It is important to him because his glory, his

mediatorial glory, is linked to your salvation. He does it not for any good in me, but for his name's sake. Bless his name!

How sweet the name of Jesus sounds
In a believer's ear!
It soothes his sorrows, heals his wounds,
And drives away his fear.
John Newton

4

Protecting the Flock

'Yea, though I walk through the valley of the shadow of death, I will fear no evil: for thou art with me; thy rod and thy staff they comfort me. Thou preparest a table before me in the presence of mine enemies: thou anointest my head with oil; my cup runneth over. Surely goodness and mercy shall follow me all the days of my life: and I will dwell in the house of the LORD for ever'—(Psalm 23:4–6)

A s we go through the last three verses of this psalm, let us remember that we are dealing with a living Shepherd and living sheep. Let us remember too that the Shepherd is also the Son, the Shepherd King, the one into whose hands are committed the salvation and the safety of those whom the Father loved with an everlasting love. What a trust the Father of eternity has in his Shepherd! And, my friend, if the Father is well pleased with him, how much more should we be! Let me remind you that a shepherd's reputation is staked upon the kind of sheep that his shepherding produces. You can tell by looking at a sheep what kind of shepherd it has.

'He leadeth me in the paths of righteousness *for his name's sake.*' The moving cause of our salvation is found not in our sin, our need, or our lostness, but in the grace and mercy flowing through the heart of our Triune God. The God who moved initially to redeem his people, to save and shepherd his sheep, will complete the job.

Let me remind you again that there is great logic in Scripture, and great logic in this psalm. 'The LORD is my shepherd,' says the psalmist, and out of that he takes the great assurance, 'I shall not want.' That is the foundation upon which the whole towering beauty of Psalm 23 is raised. It goes out of sight in the glory-land itself and finishes up in the Father's house.

Here is the logic of the psalm. You can carry its conclusions back to the suffering and death of Psalm 22 and see how naturally and logically they follow on from there. Like Paul's great statement in Romans 8:32—'He that spared not his own Son, but delivered him up for us all [that is what we have in Psalm 22], how shall he not with him also freely give us all things [that is what we have in Psalm 23]?' The one thing flows out inevitably from the other.

Talking about the Shepherd

This psalm is about the free giving of God. It is the Shepherd with his sheep. You are seeing here the Shepherd through the eyes of the sheep, through the contentment and the confidence of the sheep. And the only way really to see Christ is through the eyes of a new heart. It is the new heart that God can give us that enables us to see the beauty of Christ and to understand him as our Shepherd. It is very sad that, no matter how intelligent and sophisticated and able the unregenerate mind and heart are, they can only know *about* Jesus; they cannot really see him through the eyes of a sheep.

In the first three verses of the psalm the sheep are talking *about* the Shepherd, using these great personal pronouns 'I', 'me' and 'my'. It is wonderful to be able to talk about the Shepherd when you can say 'He is *my* Shepherd.' The sheep was talking about *recognition:* he knew the Shepherd and the Shepherd knew him; that was the basis of his confidence. He was also telling of *satisfaction,* and through the eyes of the sheep we can see how satisfied a sheep this was. And finally, he was speaking of *restoration*.

Talking to the Shepherd

Now when we come to verse 4, the psalm changes. Instead of talking *about the* Shepherd, the sheep is talking *to* the Shepherd. There is a world of difference between those two things. It is wonderful to be able to talk about God, and it is important that we do talk about God and tell out what the Lord has done for our souls. But, you know, it is more wonderful still to be able to talk *to* the Shepherd, and we can do that. We read in Hebrews 2 that 'he took not on him the nature of angels but ... the seed of Abraham.' He is one with us in nature. He has the divine nature, but he has the human nature too. This is a Shepherd who can identify with his sheep, and his sheep can talk to him. Do you talk to the Shepherd? Talk to him simply. You do not need a dictionary to learn how to talk to Christ; you only need grace, the grace of God. You do not need philosophy to learn how to communicate with God—you will never learn it through the philosophy of this world—you only need grace.

Talking to the Shepherd is very intimate. These last three verses are intimate, and I think (although I would not be dogmatic about it) that they have a particular aspect of a sheep's life in view.

This does not happen any longer in the circles in which I shepherded, but it certainly happened in David's day, and we have some parallels in our own day. At the time when the winter was ending, and when the spring rains had come on the mountains and the grass had begun to grow, the shepherds in Israel journeyed away from the plains and went with the sheep to the mountains. They were away not just for weeks, but for the whole of the summer. Do you remember when Samuel was sent by God to anoint the son of Jesse? Where was David then? He was away with the sheep, and he was away for the summer. They took the sheep up into the mountains for the summer grazing.

It was in the mountains that the lambs were born. The shepherds left their homes in the lambing season, and ewes in lamb had to be driven carefully and slowly and handled tenderly. Lambing time is a wonderful time for a shepherd. I very often used to have four collie dogs with me when I went to the hills, but in lambing time I took only one dog, a little dog called Dusk. Little Dusk was very gentle, and the sheep hardly noticed her. They knew her and I think they loved her. Dusk used to sit up on the tank of my motor-bike and hold her nose into the wind. She went everywhere I went, and it was Dusk that I would use through the weeks of the lambing. Why? Because sheep need tender handling then.

Now if a shepherd has to think of these kinds of things (and he does), how much more does our God deal tenderly with us! We have been talking a lot about revival. You are longing for revival in Wales, and you feel that it is very barren. Last night in bed I was thinking about that, and then I remembered. The shepherd moves very quietly in the hills as the lambing season approaches, and the sheep hardly notice he is there. They hardly notice he is there because (and only because) the lambing season is coming. I wondered. I wondered if what you think of as barrenness is the beginning of a great lambing season again in the churches and in the flock of God in Wales. Let us pray that it is.

Many of the commentaries that I have consulted on Psalm 23 have been disappointing. One of the things that disappointed me in them was this: they almost all said that the imagery of the psalm changes from being a shepherd with his sheep to being a general with his army. Some of them say that it changes three times: you have the shepherd with his sheep; then the traveller, the guide and his companions; and then the warfare. Now I think that all this is nonsense. It is when they come to verse 5 that the commentators get stuck: 'Thou preparest a table before me.' Oh, they say, the shepherd has gone now, and so have the sheep. Well, you don't lose a shepherd and his sheep as easily as that! I believe that the shepherd/sheep picture is sustained right through the psalm.

'Yea, though I walk ...'

But first we look at verse 4: 'Yea, though I walk through the valley of the shadow of death ...' Here we are in the valleys, and it is the valley of the shadow of death. This is a great verse; it is the hinge of the psalm. Spurgeon said of this verse that it has been a pillow, a dying pillow, to thousands of the saints of God. They have laid their heads down on it and they have passed into the Glory with calmness and assurance and confidence. He is right. I believe the verse does talk about death. Most of the commentators, including John Calvin, say that here we have life. Calvin thinks that it refers to the dark valleys through which the Christian is brought in his journey. I believe he can be right, but I don't think it stops there. I think that the psalmist is talking about the reality of physical death.

What a terrible word has come into this beautiful psalm— death! Yes, and what a terrible thing death is! What a malignant, awful thing came into God's universe when sin came into it., for sin brought forth death. What is death? It is the wages of sin; that is why it is in the psalm. But I am glad it is in the psalm, because it ties the psalm into the life that you and I have to live. It tells us what the shepherd is really concerned about, namely, the life of his sheep. It will help you and me not only to die, but to live so that we may die without fear.

The Bible talks in many places about the valley of the shadow of death. For example, when it talks about the coming of the Shepherd, it says that he came from heaven's throne to those who 'dwell in the land of the shadow of death' and 'the people that walked in darkness' (Isaiah 9:2). This is a picture of a world without God. Paul tells us, 'And you hath he quickened, who were dead in trespasses and sins' (Ephesians 2:1). You see, this Shepherd is delivering us from that death, from eternal death. This Shepherd says, 'I am the resurrection, and the life: he that believeth in me, though he were dead, yet shall he live' (John 11:25). That verse does not speak of physical death or of physical resurrection, but of spiritual death. We know this because he then goes on to say, 'Whosoever liveth and believeth in me shall never die. Believest thou this?' Of course we do! It is the truth, that is why we believe it.

That is one aspect of the valley of the shadow of death, and that is why I think John Calvin has something; because you and I will have to journey through the valleys. Most of us know far more about the valleys of Christian experience than we do about the mountain tops. But he is with us in the valleys, and he is with us in the darkest valley of all.

Death

I was hearing a testimony the other night. I was thrilled to hear it, and I am glad that many of God's people can give it. The testimony was very simple but very genuine: 'I am not afraid to go; my case is packed and I am ready.' That is wonderful. But I believe that many of God's people still know what the fear of death is. We read in Hebrews of those who 'through fear of death were all their lifetime subject to bondage' because of 'him that had the power of death, that is, the devil' (Hebrews 2:14–15). That is the bondage which Christ came to break: first of all, the fear of spiritual death; and then, also, the fear of physical dissolution, the separation of soul from body.

But I think you should not be overly concerned if sometimes you are afraid of death. I have met people who have said, 'Mr MacMillan, I am afraid I can't have Christ at all, because I am still afraid of death.' Now I have to look at this through the eyes of the apostle Paul. Paul could say, 'For to me to live is Christ, and to die is gain', and he could also say, 'having a desire to depart and to be with Christ; which is far better' (Philippians 1:21,23). But let us not forget that Paul also had to say that death was an enemy. More than this, he said it was the *last* enemy, and we praise God for that.

Can I again use personal experience? I remember the morning of the day on which my father died. Rather, it was the day before, the Saturday morning, for he died just after the entrance of the Sabbath. (He went on the Sabbath to his rest with his Master on 16 June 1957, two years and two days after I was converted.)

On that Saturday morning I was going out on to the hill early. My father had been ill for three weeks, and as I looked into his room before going out at half-past six that June morning, he was propped up on pillows looking out of his bedroom window on to a kind of long, sweeping hill that rose behind our house. He was very weak, but he looked at me and said, 'Hello, Douglas, are you going out?' When I said 'Yes', he said, 'Sit down, sit for a minute.'

Then he said, 'What do you see out of the window, Douglas?' So I looked and told him, 'Well, I see the sheep just beginning to come down.' (The sheep always go up to the top of the hills at night to sleep—and many a Christian could learn a lesson from that. Go up to the hills before you go to sleep at night.) He said, 'It's strange, you know'—and a smile came over his face. (I had noticed a strange light in his face as soon as I went into his room.) 'It's strange, you know, man. I can't see that now at all.'

I said, 'What do you see ?' He said, 'It's strange, I'm looking out of the window and it's as if I was looking into an orchard. It's a very beautiful place, and I can see people and I know a lot of them. I can see my mother and I can see your mother.' (I had lost my mother six years before.) Then he smiled again and said,

'Do you think I am seeing into heaven? I think I am.' He said, 'I have been on the doorstep for three weeks'—he had been asking people not to pray that he would get better—'and I am going to go over it today.' Then he said,

> For forty years I have followed Christ, and for forty years I have prayed for grace to live for Christ, and for forty years I have prayed for grace to die like a Christian. I have always been afraid secretly—never admitted it, but I have always secretly been afraid that I wouldn't get grace to die. But now I see how stupid I was. God wouldn't give me grace I didn't need until I needed it; and when I need it, I have it.

He said, 'Don't be afraid of death, it's going to be wonderful.'

I was with another minister two weeks before he died, a man who loved the Lord. His wife and son (also a minister) told me of their experience with him. He had been very weak, and he was a very gentle, good man, who was steeped in the Scriptures. He had not mentioned to his son or to his two Christian daughters or his wife that death was drawing near. In fact, when I was visiting two weeks before, one of his daughters (a nurse) was very concerned about him. When I asked her why she was crying she said, 'Oh, Dad had a bad night and, you know, when he got better this morning he didn't seem to realise how near death he was, and he was talking about his cabbages. Do you think there is anything wrong with my father?' (She meant something wrong spiritually.) I said, 'No, there's nothing wrong.'

They told me that two hours before he died, he sat up in bed (for days before that he had barely been able to move), and a light came on to his face and he said to his son sitting beside him, 'Get your mother, bring them all down. I am seeing into heaven and I can see the Saviour. He is with me.' His wife came down and she started to cry (who wouldn't?). But he said, 'Peggy, don't cry. This is what I have been waiting for. This is my coronation day.' He was like that until he passed into the glory that he was seeing. It is a wonderful thing to see God's people go home to the Father's house; and it is a terrible thing, on the other hand, to see people go out into eternal darkness.

Walking through

This is what the psalmist is talking about. 'Yea, though I walk through the valley of the shadow of death ...' Death is a terrible word, but there are four other words in this verse that I want to look at with you very quickly. The first one is this: he is *walking*. The sheep is still walking, and as long as a sheep is walking you know that she is not too bad. The second word is this: he is walking *through*. He does not say he is walking *in* the valley of death, but he is walking through it—and between walking in and walking through there is not only a world of difference but an eternity of difference! What does he mean? He means that already he is seeing the exit.

My mind goes back to just after we moved, five and a half years ago, from Aberdeen to Glasgow. Our youngest boy was then four years old, and just below our house was the Clyde Tunnel. It is well lit up and goes down, and then up the other side. I was going to a hospital just the other side of the Tunnel, and my wife had asked me to take the 'wee fellow' with me. 'Are we going through the Tunnel?' he said. 'Oooh! that's great!'

But when we went down into the Tunnel he must have been thinking, because he said to me, 'Is there water up there?' I said, 'Yes, there's water up there.' 'What if it comes down here, Daddy?' he said. Then his face looked very troubled and he said, 'Oh, hurry up, I don't like this place.' Just then we started to climb out of it again and he said, 'Oh, that's good, I can see the other end.'

Well, that is what the psalmist is talking about; he was *walking through*. You see, physical dissolution for the sheep of this

Shepherd, for every believer, is only a gateway, an entrance into his nearer presence.

Shadows

He is *walking,* he is going *through* the valley, and the valley is not really the valley of death, but the valley of the *shadow* of death. I think it is old Matthew Henry who says there is a great difference between shadow and substance: the shadow of a snake cannot sting you, and the shadow of a sword cannot kill you. Spurgeon quotes that in his commentary, and then he adds for himself that the shadow of a dog cannot bite you—I like that! But what difference is there between shadow and substance? All the difference in the world! Who is afraid of shadows? Only the wee boys and girls are frightened by them.

There is something else about a shadow. You never get a shadow unless there is light in the immediate vicinity. It is light that *casts* the shadow. What does that mean? Well, this is the picture I have of it. I can see the shepherd with the sheep. The sheep are walking through the valley on a little track, and by the side of the track there is the angel of death. But behind the angel of death there is something else, the light of the Shepherd's life, the light of the resurrection life of Christ. 'The Lamb is all the glory in Emmanuel's land.' The glory of the Lamb is shining out, and it is the light of the glory of the Lamb that casts the shadow. Death lies between the believer and the glory that is to be his. The glory shining out throws a shadow across the path, but all the believer has to do is to walk through the shadow; and then death is behind, and the glory is coming ever nearer.

'Thou art with me'

'Yea, though I walk through the valley of the shadow of death, I will fear no evil.' Somebody said to me last night, 'I am sure, Mr MacMillan, you have noticed that there are only two negatives in this psalm.' Well, I have been looking at this psalm a long time, but I had never particularly noticed this. How on earth did I miss them? 'I will not want', and 'I will fear no evil.' What wonderful negatives they are!

'I will fear no evil.' Why can he say this, when the enemy, the last enemy, is so near? Because *'thou art with me'*. You see, the shepherd goes with the sheep. When the sheep begins to climb the mountain (and that is what the sheep is doing here), the shepherd is with him. A sheep always gains confidence from the presence of its shepherd.

I can remember Dusk, the little sheep-dog, barking furiously one morning when we had all our young lambs down in the park in front of the house. Now Dusk hardly ever barked, but here she was barking at about half-past six in the morning, as it was just getting light. I was not very happy about this, and neither was anyone else, so I got up and went to my bedroom window intending to give her a real scolding. My eyes looked down the park, and there were two strange dogs worrying the lambs and the young sheep. That is why Dusk was barking.

Now what did I do? I went down there as quickly as I could. All these young sheep were disturbed; they had been raced all over the park. Some of them had been bitten, and there were bits of wool lying here and there. Some of them had blood on them, and they would have been slaughtered had Dusk not barked. As soon as they saw Dusk, first of all, and then me trotting along behind her, things calmed down. Why? 'Thou art with me.'

This truth could be illustrated in a thousand ways, but we do not have time to do it. Some sheep can be very tense and nervous, but the shepherd's presence calms the most nervous sheep. People often think of sheep as silly animals. Well, they are very stubborn sometimes, and of course *some* sheep can be silly, just like some people; but sheep are not silly creatures. I listened to a psychologist lecturing when I was doing my degree in Aberdeen

University. He told us that animals had no intelligence, so I went to speak to him afterwards about foxes and sheep-dogs. I don't know whether he changed his views or not, but he nodded. I think I have seen a few foxes who could outdo the psychologist!

Some sheep are by nature very nervous and tense, and some Christians are too. When we are converted, although we are given a new nature, the old nature is not taken away. We are being redeemed as individuals, and sometimes our physical make-up will affect our Christian life. But the Shepherd knows the sheep not merely as a flock but as individual sheep—and that is a blessing! The things that bother me may not be the things that will bother you, and we are very foolish to look for uniformity of experience or to want to be put in the same mould. The wonderful thing is that when we have been fashioned into the image of Christ, God still leaves in us our own individuality and our own identity. 'Thou art with me.'

The rod and staff

Then we go on to the strange words, 'thy rod and thy staff they comfort me'. Every commentator I have consulted has said that here is a shepherd going with a stick in one hand and a club in the other. Well, that may be so. (I cannot be too dogmatic, as I have never seen a shepherd working in the East.) There were times when I had to go with a .303 rifle over my shoulder, but I *always* went with what we call a shepherd's crook. You would choose a hazel stick, and would spend the winter either shaping a ram's horn to fit it, or, if you found the right kind of branch growing out of a tree, you would cut out the block and shape a wooden one. This was the shepherd's instrument for working with the sheep. I never in my life saw a shepherd go to the hills with two crooks; by the time they reached the stage when they needed two sticks, we used to say to them, 'Just you stay at home!'

This one instrument of the shepherd has many uses. He could use it as a *staff*. He could use it to pick up the little lambs—that is how one caught them when they were running away. You just hooked them around the neck and brought them up, and they would be in your hands; that is why the crook is so long. If you had a sheep stuck down in a bog or a pit, you used it to hook her out too, or at least you got your hands on her by using the stick. Or if she fell into the sea or into the river, then you hooked her out with the crook. You used it as an instrument to help the sheep. If you had to examine a sheep to see if it had scab, you would lift its fleece with your crook. Have you ever been at a sheep show and seen the judge? They are very important fellows who go around staring at the sheep. 'They've got an eye for a sheep,' the sheepmen say. You see them fluffing up the wool with their sticks. What are they doing? They are looking for scab or ticks, examining the kind of skin the sheep has, and they do it with the crook. The crook is being used as a *staff* to help the sheep.

But the crook can also be used as an instrument of defence. You used it not only to help the sheep, but also to defend and, sometimes, to correct the sheep. Then it would be used not as a staff, but as a *rod*.

It is lovely, and it warms our hearts, to think of the Shepherd, our Lord Jesus, using the crook to help us, and to be a means of blessing to us; but it is not so nice when we think of him using the crook as a rod of correction. But, my friend, we need it. Sheep need it. This is what Hebrews says: 'whom the Lord loveth he chasteneth, and scourgeth every son whom he receiveth' (Hebrews 12:6). On every son that God loves he will bring chastening, for his profit, for his sanctification, for his correction and his growth in grace.

And although we tend to think that it is nice when the Shepherd is using the crook as a staff of help, but not so nice when he is using it as a rod, you see what this sheep is saying—'thy rod *and* thy staff they *comfort* me'. How can he say that the rod of chastisement comforts him? For one reason only. The crook, the shepherd's instrument, whether it is used as a staff or a rod, is held in the same hand; it is the hand of the shepherd.

We used to have to 'handle' sheep. We had to dip them three times a year, and we would take them in 'fanks'—that is, sheeppens—and 'handle' them. That is a lovely word, and we have it in Gaelic too. The old Christian people used to talk in Gaelic and ask, 'How is God handling you just now?' By that they meant, 'What is God doing with you in the realm of the spirit and of the soul?'

I remember dipping sheep with two of my brothers. We used to get tourists even away up in Argyllshire, and when they saw sheep in a 'fank', cars would stop and the people would come over. One of them, I remember, seeing these big rough fellows picking up little sheep and tossing them about (as they thought) said, 'Oh dear! Aren't you very rough with those sheep?' There was the 'big fellow' picking up a sheep with his huge hands, and it looked as if he had just got hold of it any old way and it was hanging there. But, you see, he was holding a sheep precisely as a sheep should be held. Those big, rough hands were very tender really, and what looked like rough handling was in fact very tender handling.

Of course, the sheep did not like being shoved into a bath of strong-smelling dip and having their heads pushed right down, any more than they liked getting injections from the shepherd to stop them having fluke or what we call 'trembling'. But whether the sheep liked these things or not, they had to have them. A shepherd has to handle his sheep, and ultimately the sheep know that this is for their own good. 'Yea, though I walk through the valley of the shadow of death, I will fear no evil: for thou art with me; thy rod and thy staff they comfort me.'

God will have to bring many things into our experience that we will not like, but God's people can take comfort even from the hard things and the dark places. We are not often on the mountain tops; many of us are more often in the valleys—and, you know, a valley is a safe place. In Scotland, and I suppose sometimes in Wales too, we read all too often of young men and young women being destroyed on the mountains. They go climbing, and they fall down and get killed. Now if they had stayed in the valleys, they would have been as safe as safe could be. A valley is a safe place; you will never fall down and break your leg or your neck there. But the mountain tops are exciting. Of course, that is why they climb them. You get wonderful vistas from the mountain tops, but they are dangerous.

You know, we pray and ask God for blessing, but sometimes we do not know what we are asking for. We are asking for a lot of trouble in our hearts and in our lives; we are asking God to handle us and mould us. If you have been praying for holiness of life and restoration into his favour and fellowship, then God is going to handle you and sin is going to have to go. Perhaps you are going to have to have the rod. Ah! But, my friend, it is worth it, because it is the Shepherd who is doing it all, and he never hurts you in any way that will be to your ultimate ill, but always for your good. All things, yes, *all things* work together for good to them that love God and who have been shepherded by God's love.

The table and the enemies

Now we come to verse 5—'Thou preparest a table before me in the presence of mine enemies.' Where are we now? We are in the journeys of the sheep as they are going up into the mountains, and it may be that what the psalmist is thinking about as the 'table' is the flat plateau on the top of the mountains where lush grass grows. Just recently, however, I read something else that interested me; it was in a book about the needs of agriculture in Eastern countries. It talked about shepherding, and of how difficult it was to bring in new sheep and improve the stock because of the infestation of the sheep grounds with all kinds of parasites. And the suggestion was made that sheepmen in the East should return to an old oriental practice in their husbandry— feeding the sheep on raised tables.

When the shepherd was on the mountain, he would not go all over the mountain to hand out food to his sheep, but he would bring them to one place. The sheep would come in carrying these pests with them, and so the ground would become infested. If the shepherd put their hand-feeding down on the ground, they fed not only on the food but on the bacteria that were there. So, according to this book, the old oriental shepherding practice was to use little raised tables. (That is why shepherds in the Highlands, and probably in Wales too, use wooden troughs.) It was not just to save the food, for the sheep could get it off the grass, but it would be quite dangerous and harmful to put it on the grass in the same place every day.

This, I think, is what David is talking about. The sheep pick up these parasites, these 'enemies', and get all sorts of diseases from them, just as you and I do, although we didn't know about it until the scientists told us. These sheep were being preserved from their enemies, from that which would destroy them. 'Thou preparest a table before me in the presence of mine enemies.' I don't think the psalmist has moved away from the shepherd image at all. He is feeding his sheep in the presence of the enemies.

Or even if he is just shepherding them in the grass, he is also protecting them from their enemies. I have referred earlier to a sheep that got 'cast' or 'coped'—a sheep that had fallen over, for one reason or another, on to her side, or maybe right over on to her back, so that she could not get up and her life was in danger. One of the things that I was always afraid of, especially at lambing time, when we were looking for sheep that were cast, was that they would be attacked by hooded crows (black and grey crows) and black-backed gulls (huge sea-gulls). These birds would watch, and whenever they saw a sheep in difficulty over rising, they would fly in to attack them. It would be the same in David's time, but in David's land the birds would be vultures and buzzards.

So, going out to my sheep on the hills, one of the first things I would do was to look up into the sky, and if I saw the crows circling, then I would run. Hooded crows would pluck out a sheep's eyes, leaving her blind, and black-backed sea-gulls would go straight into her ribs for her liver. A shepherd did not like them—a sheep's life was in danger. And so the shepherd, even in our day, shepherding his sheep in the Highland hills or the Welsh hills, is in a very real sense giving them their food, laying a table before them, in the presence of their 'enemies'.

That is what God is doing. You and I do not know—we do not begin to know—the enemies that our souls have, but God knows them all, and he shepherds us, not only in order to save us but to preserve us.

One of my great fears the night I was converted was, Can I keep it up? I had discovered that God could save me, but would I be able to keep it up? They were saying in the local pub that I would not be able to keep it up. As soon as they heard I was converted—and I told them all—they were actually laying bets as to how long it would last. That was on 14 June, and in the middle of July there were Highland Games in the place, and there was the Games Dance and Concert. They were saying, 'He'll maybe make it to the Games Dance, but he'll never get past that.' And when God took me past the night of the Games Dance, they started laying bets again; but now they were giving themselves more margin and said, 'He'll maybe make it to the New Year.'

But, you see, God not only saves; he keeps. He prepares a table for us in the presence of all who would pull us down and separate us from his Shepherd-heart and Shepherd-love.

The oil and the cup

'Thou anointest my head with oil.' That means a lot to a shepherd. We used to have to bring our sheep in and make all sorts of fancy mixtures based on linseed oil. We would be anointing their horns and their heads to keep away the flies I was talking about earlier. At one time we used to have to do it every ten days, until the researchers developed better dips and sprays and anti-fly and anti-strike solutions. In my early days these things had not arrived, and nearly all the medicine was based on two things—linseed oil and 'archangel' tar (of all things!). But it worked, if you kept working at it. The oil would heal wounds, and you actually poured it over the sheep's head, because flies attack a sheep not through her thick wool but all round her head, and they are very bothersome to her. 'Thou anointest my head with oil.'

Now apply that to the Holy Spirit. It is the safe keeping of God in the anointing and blessing of the Holy Ghost that preserves us. People talk about the baptism of the Spirit and the filling of the Spirit. Well, I like to hear them talking about it. I believe that our relationship with the Spirit has to be a constant, ongoing one, and if you rest content with any one experience you begin to be finished. You need the Holy Ghost and all the grace of God available to you in the Holy Ghost today, and you need all the power of the Holy Ghost that God will grant you through him. You need an anointing, and, you see, this is what the sheep have. 'My cup runneth over': it is not just sufficient, it is abundant.

I remember the first time I ever sat at the Lord's table. I was not very long converted, and there was an old minister preaching, born and bred on the Island of St. Kilda. He was a lovely man. He had been a sailor for 40 years, and then he had studied for the ministry. God had blessed his ministry, and I think he was then about eighty-four or eighty-five years of age. He was preaching the sermon leading up to the administration, the taking, of the Supper, and his text was, 'Father, if it be possible, let this cup pass from me.' He was painting a very vivid picture. (That is the kind of man he was; he didn't bother about polishing his sermons or looking for all the fancy words, but he built eye-pictures.) He said:

Here is a Father, the eternal Father, and his hand comes down and it is holding a cup. Look at the cup, it is full, and it's full of the wrath of a holy, almighty God. And look, there's the Shepherd of the sheep, and he is stretching out his hand. He takes it and he shrinks and he draws back his hand and he looks up and says, 'Father, if it be possible'. But no, his hands go up, he is taking it and he is putting it to his lips.

Then he says, 'Do you know what he is doing? He is drinking it to the dregs.' Then he stopped for a long time, and said very quietly, 'And what's he doing with it now? He's licking it clean.' Then,

What's he doing with it now? He's filling it up, he's pouring into it and it's beginning to flow over. And what is he pouring into the cup? Eternal love! And now he is holding it out, and what's he doing with it? He's handing it to you, believer. 'This is my body, broken for you.' That's the Shepherd.

I enjoyed that preaching; I never forgot it. We don't hear much of that sort of preaching now, do we? That old man loved the Saviour and loved the Shepherd and loved the sheep too. 'My cup runneth over.'

Goodness and mercy

We come now to the last verse: 'Surely goodness and mercy shall follow me all the days of my life: and I will dwell in the house of the Lord for ever.'

Goodness and mercy. Now God is good to all his creatures; his goodness goes out even to the wicked, we are told. Isn't he a gracious, wonderful God? It is of the goodness of God that the blasphemers of our day are allowed to blaspheme his name, for they are in the hollow of his hand and none of them knows it. These thoughtless people that would never come into a preaching service here or out there on the streets, God is upholding them and they are enjoying God's goodness. He gives us rain and he gives us sunshine, not only to the righteous but to the wicked, and that goodness is given basically for his people.

Why has he not judged the earth, because he is redeeming his people from it? Ah! But it's not just goodness, it's mercy, and mercy is the goodness of God coming out to us despite our sin. Mercy is just the goodness of God to a hell-deserving sinner like you and me. Mercy is goodness that brings love— it's a lovely word! The word that is often used in the psalms is 'lovingkindness', the loving-kindness of God, and I think this combines goodness and mercy.

I remember listening to an old Highland shepherd, an elder, preaching on this verse. He was only an old shepherd, not a fancy theologian, but he was wonderful. He said:

What do I think of when I think of goodness and mercy? I think of the fellows taking the sheep home, walking down the road there with their sticks. The sheep are coming behind them, and behind the sheep are the two dogs, and one is called Goodness and the other is called Mercy.

You watch them. Sheep being what they are, when the shepherd's back is turned, they'll try and sneak off the road.

You see a sheep on one side, and off it goes trying to get back to the pasture and the mountains. Without even the shepherd whistling, what happens? Goodness runs out and circles the sheep and turns it back into the flock and into the path of God. Then, a little further along the road, another one will do the same, or two or three will do it. And there you will see Mercy running out and turning the sheep back too. Ah! they are two lovely dogs, Goodness and Mercy.

I think if I was still shepherding, and I still had two dogs, I would call one Goodness and I would call the other Mercy, because it's a very true picture. Wherever the old man got hold of it, it is a picture wonderfully true to life.

Just ask yourself this question. How often, my friend, have you strayed or tried to stray since the Shepherd first brought you into the flock? How often has it been not the judgement you were expecting and the correction that you deserved, that brought you back down off the wandering pathway to the hills, back down to the road and the pathway? Not a judgement, nor correction, but the goodness of God. And how often has it been the case that when you expected God to cast you off, his mercy has come out and touched you and brought you back into the flock? You know, it is wonderful when you are looking for the judgement of God and he visits you with mercy. It breaks your heart, doesn't it? It makes you love the Shepherd all the more. We deserve nothing but his wrath, and yet daily his goodness and his mercy are following us. David says that they follow us 'all the days of our lives'.

Some of these days are dark and difficult days. I remember being on holiday once in Tobermory, where my sister and her husband live. There were boats down from Orkney, fishing for shellfish out in the Sound of Mull. An old Orkadian had come over to my brother-in-law's garage to have something done to the engine of his boat, and he got talking with Duncan. They discovered that they were both Christians and got to know one another. Then the boats went away for a whole winter and came back again the next spring, clam-fishing. Duncan wondered if this old Christian fisherman would come along and see him, and he did. Duncan said to him, 'And how are things going?' He said:

Well, I have come through, in recent weeks, the most severe testing my faith has ever had. I have never sailed from home for any fishing ground without first of all committing myself and my crew to God. Just recently, a lovely young fellow of 16 was converted in our town. He came to me and asked for a job on the boat. I was needing someone, and what better than to have a lovely young fellow like that?

His very first time with us, we went out setting nets in a heavy swell, and something happened that has never happened to me in 40 years at sea. A net got loose and his feet got caught in it and he was over the side, and before we got him back he was drowned. Duncan, it's been dark; why did God permit it?

I thought that Duncan gave him a very wise answer. He said:

George, you and I will never really understand, though we can say this: he has gone home, and it's far better for him, and it may be that God was saving him from trials that you and I will not be spared from. We don't know, but we do know this, that God doeth all things well, and his goodness and his mercy *will* follow us all the days of our lives.

Now that includes everything, doesn't it? Every possibility, all the days. It includes the days when I am in a bad mood and am not feeling godly and pious, when I am not in a conference and people can't see me, and I don't really feel like getting down on my knees, and I don't want to open the Bible, and I am in a mood against him. Sheep can be very rebellious, and so can you! I know you because I know myself. Even in *these* days, in his goodness and his mercy he won't put his hand on us to destroy us, but he will put his hand on us to bring us back and calm us down and show us his goodness and his mercy. There is a lovely phrase in one of the psalms: 'Thy gentleness hath made me great,' said David. The gentleness of God in his dealings with us!

The Father's house

Then, 'I will dwell in the house of the LORD for ever.' His goodness and mercy have followed him all the days of his life. Those two wonderful dogs have shepherded the flock who are following the Shepherd, and at last they have guided them safely right into the gates of the Father's house. They are back home! They are where they want to be. 'I will dwell in the house of the LORD for ever.'

Then you have come into Psalm 24—'Who shall ascend into the hill of the LORD?' Our Shepherd has gone, and he has been given great glory. He is the Chief Shepherd, and by the time you reach this point in the psalm, the great characteristic of the Shepherd is that he is giving a crown of glory. His great achievement has been brought to perfection, but not to conclusion, because it will go on. This Shepherd, who is himself the Lamb, one with the sheep—this Shepherd will feed them and lead them into living fountains of water for ever. That's what it means. This same psalmist in Psalm 27 said that he longs to go to the house of God. Why? I have to quote in the metrical version:

That I the beauty of the Lord
  Behold may and admire,
And that I in His holy place
  May rev'rently enquire.

He wants to dwell in the house of the Lord and behold the beauty of the Lord and to enquire in his temple; and then the strange enigmas that have darkened our days, and the questions that have come in our hearts, will all be answered by God. 'Then shall I know'—that will be part of the leading and the feeding. Perfection? Yes! Perfection attained but perfection developing; an ongoing knowledge of the Shepherd and of the life of the eternal God. It will be wonderful!

The beauty of holiness

A phrase that has struck me and has been with me a great deal through this last winter is a very simple phrase—'the beauty of holiness'. You have heard of Robert Murray McCheyne, haven't you? A young Scottish minister in Dundee in the late 1830s, he was minister there for only five years. He was not yet 24 years of age when he went there, and he had not reached his thirtieth birthday when God took him home.

There was once a time when McCheyne was gathered with some ministers in Edinburgh, and an old Highland minister came into the home in which they were gathered. When McCheyne had left, this old Highland minister (with a lot of Christian experience behind him) looked around the other ministers and said, 'Well, well, do you know this, I have never before seen one in whom I see Christ shine as he shines in the face of that young man.'

McCheyne preached his last sermon on earth in a place outside Dundee called Broughty Ferry on a Sabbath night. He preached from the text of Isaiah 60:1—'Arise, shine; for thy light is come, and the glory of the LORD is risen upon thee.' He went home to go to bed, ill of the fever from which he was not to recover. He died just days after he had preached on that text, and after his death they found a letter under his pillow. It had come from a man who was listening to him preaching that last sermon, and in part of the letter he said this:

Dear Mr McCheyne, I heard you preach at Broughty Ferry last Sabbath evening, and your sermon brought me to Christ. It was not anything you said, but it was what you were as you preached. For as you preached, I thought that I had never seen the beauty of holiness as I saw it in you. You were talking about the glory of our God resting on the Saviour, and I saw the Saviour's glory rest on you. That brought me to Christ.

What is preaching? I don't know, but I think it rests in what a man is before it rests in what a man says. I think we can finish our whole study of Psalm 23 with a verse of a hymn McCheyne wrote:

When this passing world is done,
When has sunk yon flaming sun,
When I stand with Christ in Glory,
Looking back upon life's story,
Then, Lord, shall I fully know,
Not till then, how much I owe.

What do you owe? My friend, you owe him everything. You are only a sheep: he is the Shepherd.